D1366010

GARGANTUA

Circus Star of the Century

Gargantua by Lyn Godwin

GENE PLOWDEN

GARGANTUA

Circus Star of the Century

BONANZA BOOKS • NEW YORK

Library of Congress Catalog Card Number: 72-82924

This edition is published by Bonanza Books
a division of Crown Publishers, Inc.
by arrangement with Seemann Publishing, Inc.
a b c d e f g h
Manufactured in the United States of America

To

FREDDIE DAW,

better known as "Freddy the Clown," who insisted
I write the story of Gargantua the Great.

Acknowledgments

The fine study of Gargantua on the frontispiece of this book is the work of artist Lyn Godwin, and is published through the courtesy and cooperation of John Hurdle, curator of the Ringling Museum of the Circus, who was elected president of the Circus Fans Association of America at the 1971 convention.

My special thanks go to Tony and Clementine Desimone, who for years were associated with Gargantua's owner and who supplied many details of the gorilla's early years in this country, as well as several valuable pictures.

Photographs and lithographs in the book also came through the courtesy of the Ringling Museum of the Circus; Colonel W. W. Naramore and Dr. Bradley Kwenski of the Circus Hall of Fame at Sarasota; Don Marcks of El Cerrito, California; Paul Tharp of Loma Linda, California; Robert D. Good of Allentown, Pennsylvania; Dr. M. B. Ryckman of Saint Thomas, Ontario, Canada; Hayes Gainard of Clarklake, Michigan; Merle Evans, bandmaster, Sarasota, Florida, and his wife, Nena; the Ringling Bros. and Barnum & Bailey Combined Shows, Inc.; Freddie Daw of Circus Hobby Hall, Coral Gables, Florida, and Mr. and Mrs. Jose Tomas of Sarasota, Florida.

My sincere thanks to all of them and others who made this book possible.

GENE PLOWDEN

Miami, Florida

Contents

Illustrations

(Full color illustrations in italics)

CHAPTER ONE

Supremes of Two Centuries

Gargantua the Great was undisputed superstar of the circus in this twentieth century. Even without the "Great" in his name, the huge beast in the shaggy fur jacket was beyond question the most sensational single attraction Ringling Bros. and Barnum & Bailey Combined Shows ever had. Countless multitudes saw the gorilla billed as "The mightiest monster ever captured by man." Superlatives were showered upon him.

He was a worthy successor to Jumbo, Barnum's mammoth elephant and the biggest attraction of the nineteenth century. If these two could have appeared on the same bill, the word would have been "colossal." What a magnificent pair they would have made!

Neither was the biggest of his kind, but that didn't deter or embarrass promoters and press agents, who claimed that they were, and used generous doses of ballyhoo and bunkum to make each the most popular and profitable exhibit of his time.

If they could have trouped together, it would have been overwhelming. Imagine them on huge posters of Ringling red, canary yellow, indigo blue, and jet black; Gargantua perched high atop Jumbo's massive shoulders, jockey style; giant figures towering over thousands of patrons moving like a flood of humanity toward the ticket wagons!

Like Jumbo, who preceded him by some fifty-five years, Gargantua the Great was a star of the first magnitude, dazzling the entertainment skies. Millions stood in line through rain, wind, cold, and heat to pay admission and look at him at a time when the circus desperately needed cash to meet union demands and keep going. In his first season on tour, Gargantua saved from bankruptcy the great outdoor amusement enterprise that had thrilled and entertained Americans for more than sixty years.

Actually, Gargantua was a reluctant trouper all his life, and never performed a single trick or task to earn top billing. Yet almost overnight he became an established figure in show business, as well known as Elvis Presley and a far bigger box office sensation in the days when all America was on a spending spree along the night club and amusement circuit.

Gargantua the Great was the ugliest member of the entire ape family ever seen outside the jungles of Africa, due to an unfortunate incident, but this only enhanced his reputation as a terrifying creature. His name became a household word throughout the country, and his picture was spread around the world.

"He made good by every standard," declared Roland Butler, the astute and experienced head of the Ringling Bros. and Barnum & Bailey Combined Shows press department, who was largely responsible for making the gorilla a star. "We bill him above the humans; he earned it."

He came to the circus in a large wooden box, like a consignment of shoes or clothing, although he had not a stitch of either. He had been slipped aboard the train through a ruse, like an unwanted and unauthorized dog. The next day he was unloaded in secrecy—one of the most valuable cargoes ever to reach winter quarters of "The Greatest Show on Earth."

He arrived in Sarasota, Florida, home of the circus, on a pleasant Sunday afternoon following a 1,150-mile journey from New York City in a hot, stuffy, Seaboard Air Line Railroad baggage car.

Workmen quickly shoved the container and its contents off onto a flatbed truck backed up to receive it, and drove the three miles to quarters without guards, escort, or incident. Departure from New York and arrival in Sarasota were closely guarded secrets. Gargantua the Great was created the next day.

In its glory days, the circus grew and prospered on exaggerated claims. Both Jumbo and Gargantua were perfect specimens for promoters like Phineas Taylor Barnum and John Ringling North, respectively, to turn into cash.

Jumbo added a new word to the English language, meaning an unusually large animal or thing; so today we eat jumbo rolls, shrimp, and olives; sleep in jumbo beds; ride on jumbo tires and fly in jumbo jets.

The word "Gargantua" had been used 400 years before this unattractive ape appeared on the scene, but seldom since. Circus press agents saw the possibilities, and made it so familiar that today anything mammoth or mighty is generally considered to be gargantuan.

The huge elephant, Jumbo, created a sensation when he rode down Broadway upon arrival in this country from England in 1882.

Everything about Gargantua was magnified a dozen times. His strength, said the scriveners, equalled that of twenty-seven men. He was hailed as the most dangerous animal alive, the most terrifying creature ever captured by man, the largest gorilla ever exhibited.

None of these would stand up in the cold light of fact, but who was there to dispute the claims? The legend that no full-grown gorilla had ever been taken alive was proclaimed from billboards and broadsides. Neither was Gargantua, but such was implied.

It was reported that circus owners had given standing orders to shoot him on sight, if he ever got loose through carelessness or perhaps a train wreck, but it never happened. If it had, it would have been like shooting a house cat climbing a tree in the back yard, or a puppy cowering in a corner.

And now let's have a look at Jumbo, hailed as the largest elephant ever seen on this continent, which probably was true.

Hamran Arabs captured the elephant when he was a baby and sold him to

Johann Schmidt, a Bavarian collector, who in turn let the animal go to the Jardin des Plantes in Paris.

Some years later, the Royal Zoological Society traded a rhinoceros for him, and Jumbo went to live in the Royal Zoological Garden at Regent's Park in London. At that time he still was not unusually large–Jumbo was an African elephant and these take longer to reach maturity than their Asian cousins.

Phineas T. Barnum, who with James A. Bailey and James L. Hutchinson operated the Barnum & Bailey Circus at that time, saw Jumbo on several visits to London and decided to buy him if he could.

In the fall of 1881, Barnum sent his representative, Joseph (Joel) Edward Warner, to Europe to search for curiosities and to get anything he thought would be an attraction for the circus.

Warner said that upon his arrival in London, he visited the Zoological Gardens and, while looking over the collection, his attention was attracted to the herd of elephants.

"Several large ones met my gaze," Warner wrote in a letter dated October 11, 1906, "but towering several feet above all was the giant among the fellows, the great elephant Jumbo.

"Immediately the thought came to me that if I could secure this animal, my mission would be crowned with success. I at once entered into negotiations for this purchase.

"The monthly meeting of the Board of Fellows had just been held, and I was compelled to wait for another meeting since all sales and purchases were made by them."

Warner said that his proposal was presented while he was on the continent putting together a herd of seventeen giraffes and various other animals, and when he returned to London he found the board had decided to sell Jumbo for 2,000 pounds (roughly $10,000), "provided we would take him and make all arrangements for the shipping."

Warner, who had been elected mayor of Lansing, Michigan, in 1878 and served one term, started in show business as a magician and later became a circus official. When he closed the deal for Jumbo, news of the transaction created a hurricane of protest.

Hundreds of letters poured into London newspaper offices, many expressing indignation that a part of the British Empire was being sold to an American. Even the Queen and the Prince of Wales reportedly joined in the protest for, after all, the royal family children had ridden on his back, and he had become a popular public character.

Matthew Scott, the keeper of Jumbo (left with basket) tosses a loaf of bread into the mouth of the huge elephant.

Warner, and Barnum, stood their ground, happily waging the battle for Jumbo through the newspapers. Barnum told the London Daily Telegraph, by cablegram collect from New York, that 100,000 pounds–about $500,000–-would be no inducement for him to cancel the deal.

"Fifty million American citizens anxiously await Jumbo's arrival," the circus man claimed.

At first Jumbo refused to make the trip, and when handlers attempted to move him, he lay down in the Royal Zoological Garden. Warner reportedly telegraphed Barnum and asked what to do.

"Leave him there," came the reply. "It's worth all the publicity."

When Jumbo finally sailed for New York aboard the *Assyrian Monarch,* a British freighter, with his keeper, Matthew Scott, thousands gathered at the pier to say good-bye. It was reported that members of royalty fed the elephant cookies and wished him bon voyage while the vessel sailed down the Thames and the English Channel.

Jumbo arrived in New York on Sunday morning, April 9, 1882, to be met at the dock by Barnum, Bailey, and Hutchinson, along with members of the press and thousands of onlookers. The event had been widely publicized, but Barnum claimed he didn't know of the arrival until he read it in the morning paper!

Barnum claimed that Jumbo cost him $50,000, but it was closer to $30,000, and that included transportation and incidentals. The buildup already was under a full head of steam.

Jumbo came into the country duty free, under an agreement signed by the Treasurer of the United States, as an animal to be used for breeding purposes. The wily old Barnum didn't miss a single trick.

"How high does he reach up with his trunk–forty-nine feet, isn't it?" the showman asked the keeper.

The answer was twenty-six feet. Scott was no showman.

Reports of the day said a quart of whiskey and a quart of ale was poured down Jumbo's throat amid vigorous protests from Barnum, a teetotaler. The elephant didn't bat an eye.

"Look at the evils of intemperance!" Barnum shouted. "Why, Jumbo would have been twice as large if Scott hadn't stunted his growth by giving him a bucket of beer every day of his life."

The parade down Broadway that day, led by Jumbo and his retinue, was something to behold, as described by New York reporters in words and drawings.

Huge posters blossomed on the sides of buildings, proclaiming the new arrival as "The towering monarch of his mighty race" and "The largest animal ever exhibited." Barnum later reported that Jumbo brought the circus $336,000 in six weeks.

The largest elephant ever shot, some sources claim, was one by Jose Fenykovi, a Spaniard, in Angola, a Portuguese colony in West Africa. It measured thirteen feet two inches tall at the shoulders, and twenty-seven feet six inches from trunk to tip of tail.

Jumbo stood ten feet ten inches at the shoulders, about twenty-four feet from trunk to tip of tail, and his weight was variously reported as six, eight, or ten tons.

Jumbo was on display at Barnum's Museum or traveled with the Barnum & Bailey Circus from April, 1882, until his death on September 15, 1885.

This drawing was made for a newspaper advertisement promoting the immortal Jumbo brought to this country by P. T. Barnum, the showman.

MAJESTIC,
POWERFUL,
MASTODONIC,
WONDERFUL, **JUMBO**

A freight train struck and killed Jumbo at St. Thomas, Ontario, Sept, 1885. Reports said it took 160 men to move the carcass off the track.

The latter event put the town of Saint Thomas, Ontario, Canada, on the map, for it was here that Jumbo expired.

The *St. Thomas Journal* recalled Jumbo's death forty-two years later, commenting in 1927 that "People still talk about it as one of Saint Thomas' great events."

The newspaper reported:

"The facts are that Barnum & Bailey's circus had exhibited on the Woodworth Avenue grounds and toward the close of the evening performance the loading of elephants began.

"Thirty-one elephants had been entrained and only two remained— 'Jumbo' and another called 'Tom Thumb.' As they were being taken along the track, which the circus employees understood was being kept clear, a freight train came along.

" 'Scotty,' his keeper, made frantic efforts to get 'Jumbo' off the track but the usually docile and obedient beast balked. The keeper turned him around and endeavored to keep ahead of the train.

"They had gone thirty yards when the train hit the little elephant, which was in the rear, throwing it into the ditch and breaking its left hind leg. The train then ran into 'Jumbo,' who was crushed beneath the engine. He was terribly injured and died fifteen minutes later.

"The engine was badly damaged, the cowcatcher, headlight and bell being knocked off, and the side gear twisted. About 160 men were needed to pull the body of 'Jumbo' off the tracks. He weighed ten tons.

"Thousands of people flocked to see the body next day. The carcass was dressed by Peter Peters, butcher, and the hide and frame were turned over to the Smithsonian Institution at Washington.

"An action for $100,000 damages was subsequently brought against the Grand Trunk Railroad by Barnum & Bailey, but just before the trial was due to begin in New York City, a settlement was effected, the railroad company paying $5,000 and granting the circus free transportation over their lines the following year."

Three days after Jumbo died, Barnum wrote to Harper Brothers, book publishers, saying that "millions of children and adults are mourning the death of Jumbo," and asking if they would like to publish the life history and death of the elephant written by him.

"We think it might be a successful venture and would like to see the manuscript," the publishers replied, "if you will employ someone, accustomed to writing for publication, to prepare the book, retaining your name on the title page."

That apparently miffed Barnum, who had written several volumes about his life, and a book called *Humbugs of the World.* He never replied to Harper's proposal.

With Jumbo gone, Barnum bought an elephant named "Alice" from the Royal Zoological Society, and exhibited her as "Jumbo's widow." The public was not too impressed or responsive.

In August, 1971, Saint Thomas held a *charivari* or shivaree, and used Jumbo as its theme. A life-size model was drawn through the streets during a parade, and residents were reminded that several items pertaining to the great elephant were still on display in the city's museum, including a piece of an ear.

The importation and exploitation of Jumbo certainly was one of the showman's greatest achievements, eclipsing the Jenny Lind tours of the 1850s. Barnum reported total receipts from Miss Lind's 95 concerts amounted to $712,161.34, from which he paid the "Swedish Nightingale" $176,675,09, leaving himself $535,486.25.

All Jumbo received, in addition to his daily ration of hay and bits of grass, plus his beer or whiskey and water, was peanuts.

Mrs. Gertrude Lintz holds Buddha, a tiny, maimed baby gorilla which she bought and nursed back to health. Buddha later became Gargantua the Great.

Massa, at 41 the oldest gorilla in captivity, shown in his quarters at the Philadelphia Zoo, where he has been for 36 years.

CHAPTER TWO

An Orphan Finds a Home

Unlike Jumbo, Gargantua the Great was completely unknown when he arrived in America, without advance publicity or recognition of any kind. He was a baby, an orphan, and, in the eyes of his owner, a ruined bit of merchandise.

The owner was Captain Arthur Phillips, in command of the *West Key Bar,* a ship in the African trade. In 1928, Phillips had sold three chimpanzees which he brought from Africa to Mrs. William Lintz, animal-loving wife of a Brooklyn doctor of internal medicine.

Then in September, 1931, when the Martin Johnsons were on their way home to add two gorillas to those two already in this country, Phillips called on Mrs. Lintz again.

This time the skipper apologized for his consignment, which consisted of six young chimpanzees and a tiny bundle of hair, skin, and bones—a baby gorilla near death with double pneumonia. Mrs. Lintz took the unconscious gorilla home and for five days nursed it and fed it with a medicine dropper.

She named the baby gorilla Massa, which is Pidgin English for "Master" or "Big Boss." It lived on cereal spooned into its mouth and raw eggs and milk poured down its throat. The little ape could not chew solid food, so Mrs. Lintz masticated its fruit and vegetables before passing them on to the animal.

She kept this up for a year, and also fed it vitamins in the form of cod liver oil, later adding meat and liver to the diet. When the gorilla fell ill from what apparently was infantile paralysis, Mrs. Lintz rigged up an exercising arrangement using ropes and pulleys. The gorilla gradually regained the use of its arms and legs.

Mrs. Lintz said Massa had no hair when the baby gorilla came to her, but soon pure white hair began to grow in. Then black hair commenced to grow, giving Massa a beautiful silver-gray coat.

Three months after Massa became a member of the Lintz menagerie, Captain Phillips called his good friend, Mrs. Lintz, from Boston, first stop for the *West Key Bar* on its journey from Africa to New York.

It was just after Christmas, 1931, and this time Phillips said he was bringing in the healthiest little gorilla he had ever seen, but it had met with a horrible accident, and he was afraid it wouldn't live to reach her.

When the ship came in, Mrs. Lintz was waiting at the pier. The baby gorilla was cowering in a dark corner of the hold—a quivering, frightened creature in a strange, hostile environment.

Mrs. Lintz called for a flashlight and an empty box. Then she climbed down into the hold. When the light picked it out, the terrified little ape rushed at her. She dropped the box over it.

The story is that the latest arrival, taken as a month-old, harmless orphan, had lived with a missionary couple for about a year, then was sold to Phillips for a reported $400.

Mrs. Lintz was told that a sailor discharged when the *West Key Bar* reached Boston sought revenge on the skipper. He knew that the gorilla was a rare and valuable import, so he decided to take out his wrath by destroying it.

He slipped back aboard, emptied a fire extinguisher full of nitric acid in the gorilla's face, and left it for dead. The acid burned hair, skin, tissue, and even affected muscles of the head and chest.

"There was no question in my mind about whether I could cure him," Mrs. Lintz said later. "I had to cure him and make the world over for him, so he would know what a kind race it was that had adopted him; so that he could get back his faith in people. This effort of mine was to prove the greatest boomerang in my life—because it succeeded.

"It was a case for plastic surgery, so I called in a dermatologist. He was not able to close his eyes, and I had to put drops in them three times a day. It is a tribute to the gorilla's intelligence that after the first panic, he cooperated in his own cure.

"I really believe that he understood all the pain and discomfort was meant to help him, and the only resentment that remained in his mind was he did not trust men. He made up his mind that he would trust me, and a friendliness grew between us."

She called her youngest gorilla (then about eighteen months of age, weighing twenty-two pounds) Buddha, after the founder of Buddhism, but he generally was known as Buddy during the six years he lived in the Lintz home. Buddy and Massa were to enliven the Lintz menagerie for many eventful years.

Born Gertrude Davies in England, Mrs. Lintz was a remarkable woman. She had a life-long devotion to animals and started breeding and showing St. Bernards at Long Branch, New Jersey, in 1909. She registered her kennel, Hercuveen, with the American Kennel Club in May, 1910, and four years later swept honors at the prestigious Westminister Show in New York, and at many other shows around the country.

A keen rivalry developed between her and Colonel Jacob Ruppert, Jr., the beer baron and owner of the New York Yankees baseball team. They competed often, but the colonel's dogs never could quite match her St. Bernards. He called Gertrude "Princess."

After their honeymoon trip to Europe in 1914, Dr. William Lintz and his bride settled in a mansion on the Shore Road overlooking the Narrows of New York harbor.

Gertrude Davies Lintz, an energetic and tireless woman, was large but well proportioned, and was described by friends and employees as a "wonderful, beautiful woman."

She transformed the rambling old house and its two acres of grounds, modernizing the room plan, adding sun porches, and setting up an apartment, including a kitchen, in the basement for her staff.

Her interest in gorillas originated in 1915 during a visit to the Ringling Bros. Circus in Madison Square Garden, where she saw a baby gorilla that was ill.

"I had the feeling that if only I could take that lonely little gorilla, I could love it back to health," she said. "When it died, I felt it could have been prevented."

Years later, John Ringling, one of the five brothers who founded the famous circus bearing the name, echoed her thoughts. He told her that circus officials were hoping and praying that a woman would volunteer to nurse the little gorilla back to health.

"We had the feeling that only a woman capable of giving it real tenderness could save the youngster's life," the circus man said, "but we didn't even dare ask anybody. We felt there were too many taboos." John Ringling was a sensitive man. He realized in 1915 that the very thought of a woman caring for a gorilla might be repulsive, and he wanted no part of anything that could be considered in bad taste. This always has been a circus maxim.

Tony Desimone, who worked with Mrs. Lintz, and handled her dogs, pigeons, rabbits, chimpanzees, and gorillas.

John Ringling also loved animals, not alone for the money they brought him through the circus. He often walked about the grounds of his palatial residence in Florida or sat around the house with a pet monkey on his shoulder or by his side.

From breeding and showing St. Bernards, Mrs. Lintz branched out to include imported pigeons and rex rabbits, the latter a mammal bred without guard hair in the fur, sometimes known as chinchilla, blue or ermine rex.

When a friend presented her with a year-old chimpanzee, she began to give more and more time to these interesting primates, and eventually acquired two of their cousins, baby gorillas.

Working with her was Richard Kroener, a former butcher boy who became a kennel expert, and for twenty years was what she described affectionately as "The man at my right hand." Kroener was a born naturalist and lover of animals who collected tropical fish and butterflies, grew prize dahlias, and studied bird life.

Also with her was Anthony J. Desimone and his pert, blue-eyed wife, Clementine. Tony Desimone became one of the leading authorities on St. Bernards, and groomed the dogs for the show ring.

"He was one of the attractions of my Hercuveen bench," Mrs. Lintz said, "and thousands of people came year after year just to see Tony, with his handsome, smiling face. He was a master of the art of presenting animals at their best."

Tony went along when Mrs. Lintz began training and showing chimpanzees and became an expert in their care and handling, aided by Clementine, whom Mrs. Lintz called "Girlie."

The Desimones now live in a comfortable old house surrounded by flowers and fruit trees in North Miami, Florida, where Tony does some taxidermy but spends many happy hours reminiscing, with "Girlie" by his side. With them is her mother, Mrs. Rachel Uhl, a lively 97-year-old.

Mrs. Lintz never revealed the price she paid for the baby gorilla called "Buddy," but she said Captain Phillips "thought his value was ruined and sold him to me cheap."

Tony Desimone says she paid $2,000 for the baby gorilla and "seven or eight sickly chimps."

"I mean they were really sickly," he adds. "Dick and I got a skin disease from handling them. I went with Mrs. Lintz to get them off the boat.

"Buddy was just a little thing. I judged him to be maybe one and a half or two years old—he had no birth certificate—and he looked like a piece of raw beefsteak.

"We built cages for these animals in the basement, and they had the very best of food and care."

Mrs. Lintz oiled and massaged Buddy's skin and tissue, allowing his wounds to heal slowly. Within six months his sight had been restored, his wrinkles around the eyes were gone, and his face was smooth and unlined, like that of a young boy.

Buddy's nostrils were very flat and they almost disappeared with his injury. His mouth was drawn up on the left side, exposing some teeth and giving him the pronounced and permanent sneer that was to become his trademark—probably the most valuable animal sneer in recorded history.

"He was just the sweetest little thing," his owner reported, adding she found him utterly harmless, and even taught him to balance himself on his legs, so he could stand and walk upright like a man and feel easy on his feet with his hands in the air.

She accomplished this by teaching him to hold fruit in his armpits. He soon learned that if he relaxed his arms he would drop the fruit.

On one occasion Buddy used a chair to climb up and snitch some of Kroener's prize tropical fish. When he was turned loose in the back yard, he would search for insect eggs, caterpillars, and other morsels of gorilla food, including worms.

This gave Mrs. Lintz an idea. She began feeding him boiled liver, first cutting it into thin strips like worms. She increased his liver ration to a quarter and later a half pound a day, adding a small quantity of good ground beef to his diet every few days.

Buddy and Massa were fed three times a day, with occasional tidbits in between. They ate nothing but the best, including milk, liver; bananas,

ROPERTY
OF
S.M.U.
TH_ETIC DEPT.

apples, pears, and other fruit; lettuce, celery, and sweet potatoes; cereal and raisin bread. Tony says they liked the bread, but when they'd had enough, they would pick out the raisins and throw the bread away.

They slept eight hours a night, with often a nap in the afternoon, and Buddy gained a hundred pounds in his first year. He learned to climb trees but never ventured far off the ground, while the chimpanzees would scurry to the top of the tallest tree on the place.

Buddy never liked having his arms in sleeves, but Tony put overalls on him for short periods of time. He favored clothes to drape over his body or tear apart, and he was rather mischievous.

Tony recalls that when anyone grasped the bars of his cage, Buddy would sidle up to them very quietly and try to pin the hands against the bars, so he could grab them by arms or body.

"He was very tricky, and he learned fast," Tony says. "One time I walked too close to his cage; he reached out, grabbed my shirt, and tore it off my back. Luckily it tore easily. He was just like a big old dog. He had no use for Dick or me, but Mrs. Lintz could handle him.

"Once he was in his cage and I was saying something to Mrs. Lintz outside and I put my hand on her. Buddy saw it and he went berserk, beating on the bars and trying to break out to get at me. As he grew older, he got more resentful."

The Lintz household was always alive with dogs, fish, birds, and chimpanzees. Gray squirrels played in the back yard, and Buddy shared his food with them.

Mrs. Lintz took Buddy and Massa for rides in her car occasionally. She found they didn't mind other automobiles, but large trucks and streetcars sent them into quivering tantrums.

Buddy would sit beside his mistress with one hand on her arm and the other clutching the steering wheel. When a truck, bus, or streetcar pulled alongside, he'd yell and cover his eyes or bury his face in her dress. He also was afraid of horses.

Mrs. Lintz said she found the gorilla superior to the chimpanzee in both intelligence and emotional development. She noted the gorilla had great dignity and reserve, but his aloofness and independence kept him from becoming a useful guinea pig.

"I couldn't see it," Tony says. "I've got a lot of respect for the chimps.

Strong and tricky is the way Tony Desimone describes Buddha, who became Gargantua the Great. The gorilla never knew how strong he really was, according to Tony.

They can figure things out, and try to outsmart you. Chimps won't work for nothing—you have to reward them. The older chimps get mean. I consider the chimpanzee the most dangerous of all animals.

"The best one we ever had was Sammy; he weighed 229 pounds. I'd sooner face lions and tigers than an enraged chimp."

Tony says they never could tell if Buddy and Massa were males or females, but Mrs. Lintz thought Massa was a female.

Massa liked to imitate people, and actually learned to scrub the corners of his cage. It almost cost Mrs. Lintz her life. The gorillas and chimpanzees were being shown at the World's Fair in Chicago at the time.

Mrs. Lintz entered the room where Massa was kept, and slipped on the wet floor, dumping a pail of water on the gorilla. The startled Massa, thinking he was being attacked, leaped upon his fallen mistress and bit her savagely.

Not until a woman in the next room rushed in and clubbed Massa on the head with a heavy iron skillet did he let go. Mrs. Lintz went to a hospital, where it took sixty-five stitches to close her wounds.

From that day on, she did not trust Massa, and soon sold the 140-pound gorilla to the Philadelphia Zoological Garden for $6,000.

Mrs. Lintz herself drove the station wagon from her home in Brooklyn to the zoo on that snowy morning, December 30, 1935, and delivered what she believed to be "a female mountain gorilla" as a mate for one named Bamboo.

The strange courtship in the zoo made headlines, and it wasn't until months later that zoo officials announced they had discovered, much to their surprise, that Massa also was a male!

Bamboo lived until January 21, 1961, when he died of a heart attack at age thirty-four. He had been at the zoo for a little over thirty-three years—a record for his species in captivity at the time. He reportedly weighed 435 pounds in his prime, but this was only an estimate. At his death he weighed 281.

Massa, believed to have been born in January, 1931, is still alive as this is written, and celebrated his forty-first birthday in January, 1972.

Frederick A. Ulmer, Jr., curator of mammals at the zoo, said Massa weighs 350 pounds, somewhat less than the normal captive weight for a gorilla of his size, adding that zoo officials were trying to keep his weight down due to his age.

A recent survey showed there were at least 219 gorillas in captivity throughout the world, and Massa holds the record for longevity.

CHAPTER THREE

The Gorilla Must Go

Life was never dull around the Lintz home, and the gorilla named Buddy helped enliven it for Dick Kroener, Tony and Clemmie Desimone, and the Lintzes.

"He would put his back to the bars of his cage, so we could tickle and scratch him," Tony said. "Then he'd turn around very fast, and try to grab us.

"We used a lot of tricks to confuse him, and keep him guessing. We traveled all over with him—to Chicago, to Miami, to Atlantic City, even Toronto.

"When we would try to shift him to one end of his traveling box to clean it, we'd put in a partition. He'd always push the partition door back at us.

"We used a harmless snake to scare him into one end of his cage. He fell for this a couple of times, then one day he grabbed the snake and smashed it with his hands and feet.

"We had a steel hoe we used to clean his box. Once he grabbed that and twisted it like a pretzel. I finally got it away from him and straightened it out.

"The next time I used it, I stuck it in the furnace and let it get good and hot. Then I put it in the cage where Buddy could reach it. He grabbed it, just as I expected, but he let go of it fast and would never touch it again."

Buddy not only liked to surprise humans, he liked to snatch their clothes off. The first time he did this was in Chicago, where his victim was his owner and best friend.

They were at the Century of Progress Exposition, and Mrs. Lintz went into the cage to talk to a group of people gathered outside. As she turned to lock the door, she felt a tug and her bright summer dress was ripped off, leaving her in her slip, while Buddy draped the dress over his hairy body!

Another time, in Toronto, Buddy suddenly tore the back out of a new suit one of her helpers had just bought to wear on tour.

Again, in Miami, Buddy whipped an arm out of his cage and grabbed a railroad official by the coat and seat of his trousers. The suit came off in two furry hands. The gorilla happily flung keys, money, and papers in all directions while the startled victim ran for cover.

Buddy made periodic trips around the country with other members of the Lintz menagerie. On one of these, in Toronto, Tony was attempting to coax him into a smaller case from his cage. The gorilla turned on him.

"I always carried a blackjack," Tony recalled. "I saw him put his head and shoulders up to come for me, and I let him have it. He fell into the box.

"Mrs. Lintz came running over, and she said, 'Tony, you've killed him.'

"I said, 'It was either him or me.' "

It was during a stay in the North Miami Zoo, owned and operated by her old friend, Guarling F. Sirman, that Mrs. Lintz almost lost Buddy. It was in the fall of 1936, and again man's inhumanity was to blame, in a case paralleling that on the *West Key Bar.*

Mrs. Lintz hired a drifter looking for work to clean up around the cages. Sirman, a zoologist and herpatologist who now lives in retirement in West Palm Beach, had operated his zoo at Opa-Locka and later moved it to North Miami. He insisted that everything be kept shipshape.

The drifter hung around for a couple of days but was entirely unsatisfactory, so Mrs. Lintz fired him. That night he returned with a bottle of strong disinfectant mixed with chocolate syrup, and slipped it to Buddy in his cage.

The acid burned the lining of stomach and intestines. Even after analyzing contents of the almost empty bottle found lying outside the cage, doctors didn't know how badly the membranes had been burned—whether they might heal or if the gorilla would starve to death.

They couldn't give him glucose injections to keep up his strength; they couldn't even examine him closely. The only thing left to do was give him a healing powder, in just enough water to wash it down his throat.

Again Mrs. Lintz nursed the gorilla back to health, staying with him day and night, softly weeping at his pain and suffering, and comforting him as much as she could. She said he lost eighty pounds, and it was five weeks before she could put him back on his old diet.

During another stay in Florida, Buddy broke out of his cage and wandered off among the scrub palmettoes and pines. Mrs. Lintz and her helpers

Gargantua stared at the public from this gaudy poster after he joined Ringling Bros. and Barnum & Bailey Circus in December 1937.

Gargantua the Great and M' Toto were featured as Mr. and Mrs. Gargantua the Great after their "wedding" in February of 1941.

tracked him down, and she slowly and patiently lured him back to his cage, using a pan of milk!

On the way home to Brooklyn, they stopped off in Atlantic City for an appearance at the Steel Pier. There Maggie, a chimpanzee weighing nearly 200 pounds, escaped from her cage. This old and cantankerous chimp gave her handlers and Mrs. Lintz a solid hour of anxiety before she was captured.

Back home in Brooklyn, life settled into something of a rut, but not for long. One night a terrific thunderstorm with seventy-mile winds thrashed through the Lintz property, giving Buddy a terrible case of nerves. Somehow, the gorilla slipped out of his quarters in the basement, ambled up the stairs quiet as a shadow, and slipped into Mrs. Lintz' bedroom.

A severe clap of thunder rattled the rafters and awakened Mrs. Lintz. She was startled to find the huge, hairy gorilla lying in bed with her!

Petrified at first, she slid quietly to the floor, talking to Buddy in soft, soothing whispers. Then she tiptoed, still barefoot, to the door with her hand locked in his.

She continued to speak softly while they inched their way past Doctor Lintz's bedroom, then down the stairs to the first floor, and finally to the basement.

In the hallway, she saw a bowl of fruit and with her free hand snatched up a pear, holding it behind her until they reached his cage. She tossed the fruit inside, and Buddy ambled after it.

Next morning she told Kroener and Desimone that Buddy was outgrowing his quarters, and suggested his cage be moved into an outbuilding with stout metal doors.

She never mentioned her experience with Buddy during the storm, but she couldn't put it out of her mind. Without provocation or warning, Buddy might do the same to her or someone else that Massa had done in Chicago.

For nearly six years she had given this hairy creature motherly affection and care, but the bedroom episode convinced her that he was a grown and potentially dangerous beast. Although he had never harmed her, she concluded it was time for him to go.

Brooklyn N. Y.
December, 4, 1937

Mr. John Ringling North.
37 East 64th St.
New York.
N. Y.

Dear sir:-

For one dollar and other valuable considerations I hereby give to you for the period of one week an option to purchase for the sum of ten thousand dollars ($10,000 xx/100) my gorilla named Buddha and my two chimpanzees named Johnny and Maggie and the three steel cages two on trucks and one on a trailer now at the North Miami Zoo at North Miami, Florida. The price of the cages & trucks is not included in the price of $10,000.xx

Very truly yours,

Gertrude Davies Lintz

Agreement, drawn up by Mrs. Lintz, to sell Buddha to John Ringling North, president of the circus which made Gargantua a star and which he saved from bankruptcy.

CHAPTER FOUR

A Harmless Little Monkey

Mrs. Lintz's gorilla was known to animal trainers everywhere, and circuses and zoos throughout the country would be happy to have him. Already he had lived in captivity for more than six years, was believed to be acclimated, nearing maturity, and approaching full sexual development.

There were fewer than a dozen gorillas in the country at the time, and man's knowledge of these rare simians was extremely limited.

Buddy's owner wanted him to have the best care and attention possible, but she also hoped to get a fair price. Naturally, she thought of the Ringling Bros. and Barnum & Bailey Circus.

She telephoned John Ringling North, whom she knew, at his hotel in New York. At that time North was angling for control of the gigantic outdoor amusement enterprise operated successfully so many years by his late uncles, the five founding Ringling brothers.

North and his younger brother, Henry Ringling North, worked together and both were there when Mrs. Lintz called. She told them she had a full-grown gorilla she wanted to sell, and asked if they would be interested.

She assured them the ape was healthy, and estimated his weight at more than 400 pounds. She said his real name was Buddha, but everyone knew him as Buddy.

On that night early in December, 1937, Johnny North owned only seven percent of the circus stock, but he was an executor of the vast estate left by his uncle John Ringling, who had died just a year earlier.

North was a born showman, had traveled with the circus and worked for his uncles, had excellent financial connections, and most of all was a wheeler-dealer in the pattern of his late Uncle John.

When he hung up the phone, both Norths were thrilled at the prospect of owning a full-grown gorilla and one of the few in captivity.

"Buddy, we've just got to have that gorilla," Johnny North reminded his younger brother over and over as they rode in a taxicab toward the Lintz mansion in Brooklyn, where they'd been invited to have tea and see the big ape.

He recalled that his Uncle John had imported a couple of gorillas but neither had lived very long. One died while still very young and the other, named John Daniel and a fair-sized specimen, reportedly had cost the circus $30,000.

The show had been without a gorilla for many years, although it carried a huge menagerie, and the Norths reasoned that the time was ripe to feature one of these rare animals from Africa.

"It will be a tremendous attraction," John North reminded his brother. "If we don't grab it, someone else will. We surely don't want that to happen."

"All right, we'll buy it," Henry Ringling North agreed, "but there's one thing I insist. We're not going to have a vice-president of the circus and a gorilla both going under the name of Buddy. We'll just have to call the beast something else."

Johnny North admitted that Buddy, his brother's nickname, was not an appropriate handle for the gorilla he intended to buy, and asked Henry what he thought would be a suitable name.

Buddy North, recalling his classical studies at Yale, thought a moment and answered, in all seriousness, "Let's call him Gargantua."

This was the name of the hero of a satirical romance, "Gargantua and Pantagruel," written in 1535 by Francois Rabelias. In the story, Gargantua was a gigantic king, educated according to the noblest ideas of the humanist renaissance, and noted for his enormous physical and intellectual appetite.

After tea and considerable conversation with the lively and entertaining Mrs. Lintz, the brothers were led out to the converted outbuilding to see the object of their visit. The gorilla was housed in a sturdy cage with a sliding, slotted door.

One look at the shaggy beast called Buddy, sneering at them in the gloom of his prison, and the North brothers were ready to buy. All they needed to know was the price and date of delivery.

Mrs. Lintz said she wanted $10,000–which was to be a well-kept secret–and would draw up a simple bill of sale, terms of which were discussed.

The paper, dated December 4, 1937, was mailed to North at his New York address. In it she gave the circus man a week's option to buy the gorilla, listed under his name, Buddha.

Included in the sale also would be a fourteen-year-old chimpanzee named Maggie Klein, a member of the Lintz menagerie for thirteen years, and a young chimp named Johnny. Chimps were fairly plentiful and inexpensive.

Mrs. Lintz stipulated that the price would not include the three steel cages, two on trucks and the third in a trailer at the zoo in North Miami, Florida, that were to be provided.

During negotiations, Mrs. Lintz outlined several conditions or recommendations, some of which she repeated in the bill of sale. One was that Buddha was to be housed in a cage of her own design. Another was that Richard Kroener, who was single at the time but later married, would go with the gorilla as keeper.

"Dick was not only willing to go with Buddha, and take care of him as long as he lived, but he would have been wretched at any idea of separation," Mrs. Lintz wrote in her book, *Animals Are My Hobby,* published in 1942 by Robert M. McBride & Company.

"The two had one of the strangest relations that can be imagined. Though Buddy had cultivated his childish grudge against Dick until it became frozen into an attitude of waiting for the chance to kill him, he nevertheless trusted Dick implicitly."

The price almost matched that paid for Jumbo—chimps being fairly cheap and the two included as an afterthought—but the similarity ends there. While one was famous and a tremendous drawing card, the other was known only to a handful of animal fanciers.

Instead of coming out with a burst of publicity, as Barnum had done, the North brothers realized they must play it differently. First, the gorilla already was in New York, was virtually unknown to the public, and they'd need time to build him up as an attraction.

Second, automobile traffic had forced parades off the streets, and the circus wouldn't be in town until March.

Gladwyn Hill, New York bureau manager of the Associated Press, learned of the sale and was ready to break the story, but his friends the Norths asked him to hold off and explained why. Mrs. Lintz gave full cooperation.

If the A.P. carried the story, it would be on a spot basis, a one-shot thing, and the edge would be off. The future of Buddha, or Buddy, must be carefully planned and put in the hands of a skillful press agent, who would contrive to keep the story alive and milk it for every inch of space and radio time it would bring.

The Norths decided they would send the gorilla to winter quarters in utmost secrecy. They'd let the circus press department, headed by the resourceful and imaginative Roland Butler, take it from there.

They promised Hill they'd give him first crack at the story nationally when they were ready to release it, and immediately arranged to send the gorilla and his keeper south on the Seaboard's Orange Blossom Special, a fast passenger train between New York and Florida.

They assured Frank Eagan, the stationmaster and a long-time friend of their late Uncle John, that the big wooden box held "a harmless little monkey who needs a lot of room." They insisted it was a proper package for the baggage car.

On his last day in the Lintz home, Buddy was fed all the things he liked best, and Mrs. Lintz herself rubbed his coarse black coat with cream of petroleum.

That afternoon the big box was loaded onto a truck for the drive to the Pennsylvania Station. Mrs. Lintz went along, according to her own account tearful and whispering over and over to her pet that he was "going to Florida," assuring him that Dick was going with him and would be there to wake up "my dear Buddy" every morning.

She stood beside the bulky wooden box as it was shoved into the baggage car in violation of railroad rules against carrying dangerous animals on passenger trains.

Eagan, standing nearby, took one look inside and realized he had been tricked, but just then the whistle blew and the train pulled out. The Norths winked at him and smiled farewell.

Nearly 24 hours later, on Sunday afternoon, December 12, 1937, the hulking gorilla was unloaded in Florida sunshine, in utmost secrecy.

In those days I was sports editor of the *Sarasota Daily Tribune* and met nearly all incoming trains looking for news. There was always the likelihood that some prominent person would be aboard—a baseball, football, or golfing personality, nationally syndicated columnist, noted author or cartoonist, or perhaps one or more circus officials or performers.

Local news in our town of some 7,000 people was hard to come by, so we touched all bases in our efforts to make the paper interesting and build circulation.

"That's just another monkey we bought for the circus," the North brothers assured us as the big wooden box was moved onto the back of a truck and hauled off to winter quarters. Nobody else, including the station agent, would say anything.

We did learn that it was a gorilla, and our paper printed a three paragraph item about it next day. It was to be some weeks before Buddha or Buddy was transformed into Gargantua the Great.

When Gargantua arrived in winter quarters at Sarasota, Florida, he was housed in this steel prison and shielded from the public until the ballyhoo began.

CHAPTER FIVE

The Making of a Star

One morning Roland Butler, the great circus press agent who worked closely with Sarasota newspaper men, telephoned Earl Stumpf, a veteran of the profession and our managing editor at *The Tribune.*

Butler, who always called himself a press agent and abhorred so-called "journalists" and "public relations men," told Stumpf the circus was ready to release the story of Gargantua, the gorilla.

Stumpf, who'd had considerable theatrical and promotional experience, was delighted, of course. He had held off the story until the circus was ready. After all, the show was about the biggest thing in town; we had always given it ample coverage in our news columns and were happy to cooperate. Stumpf promised to put someone on the story immediately.

I was writing sports and features at the time, and since my sports section had already gone to the composing room, the editor suggested I go with Ned Roberts, a fellow newsman who later worked for the U.S. State Department in Washington, to winter quarters.

Roberts and I had worked closely with Butler, Frank Braden, Allen Lester, Dexter Fellows, and others in the press department. We had written many features about the circus, not only for our newspaper but for the circus' publications, and we had many friends among circus personnel.

We drove directly to Butler's musty old office in the press car, a converted Pullman once used by Al Ringling. The brass railing still guarded the rear platform, but the inside was filled with desks, typewriters, filing cabinets, and a slanted, waist-high table where Butler did his artwork. Butler was leaning over the table and Braden was at his desk when we knocked on the door.

Roland Butler, noted circus press agent, used words, pictures and drawings to make Gargantua the Great the biggest drawing card ever exhibited by any circus.

Butler, who had been an artist and entertainment editor on Boston newspapers before entering the world of sawdust and spangles, was a blocky, blue-eyed man with stentorian voice, colorful vocabulary, and mind like a dictionary.

"Come in," he bellowed, putting aside paint brushes and reaching for his gray fedora. "We'll go right over and see the gorilla. Oh, he's a pip; wait'll you see him!"

The winter quarters bristled with activity as always when the circus was at home. Elephants were shunting long, silver-sided railroad cars into the mammoth shed to be painted; wagons and trucks were jammed into the paint barns.

Downstairs in the big, three-story main building, wild animals paced or dozed in their cages; the hippopotamus wallowed in his pen, and half a dozen great polar bears in shaggy white coats cavorted in their wire-fenced enclosure.

Giraffes stretched their necks to get at weeds or grass outside their pens, or reached up to nibble at tender pine needles. Birds chirped and sang in their aviary, and monkeys chattered incessantly.

Elephants not working tugged and nipped at bales of hay in their kraals, while out back scores of horses whinnied and snorted; a dozen zebras grazed in silence, their striped coats glistening in the sun.

We passed the old Pullman that had been converted into a business office, and walked into the tent being used as a hospital. There we met Richard Kroener and his gorilla.

There was a slight chill in the air and the gorilla huddled in a corner of his cage, an old blanket spread across his legs and draped over a massive shoulder. He was slowly peeling a banana, licking and looking at it. He stopped and peered intently at his visitors.

Butler, his mind working like a computer, eyes sparkling with delight, and hat pulled down on his head, studied the latest attraction for a moment or two, then turned to Kroener and said:

"Pretty mean animal, ain't he, Mr. Kroener." It was more a statement of fact than a question for the keeper.

"No sir, Mr. Butler," Kroener replied. "He's very gentle."

"Gentle!" Butler roared in disbelief. "Why, he's the most terrifying creature on earth; a fiendishly ferocious brute. My God, he even looks mean; a real monster of the jungle. What's his name?"

"Buddha. He's nice gorilla; we call him Buddy."

"Buddy!" again Butler's voice roared through the tent and sent sidewalls flapping. "What a hell of a name for a gorilla. A terrible monster like this–Buddy! We've got to give him a new name–something to fit his size and personality, you see?

"Gargantua! That's it–Gargantua the Great. Why, he's mean as all getout. Forget that 'Buddy' stuff. We'll make him mean; feed him raw meat; get him a tire to cut his teeth on–a great big tire, you understand? My God, has he got any teeth?"

"Yes sir, He's got teeth," Kroener chuckled. "His teeth are almost like yours or mine, only much bigger. You can't see them, but he's got tusks, like big eye teeth, farther back in the mouth, to tear the meat. He's very strong, too."

"I'll say he's strong, like an ox," Butler agreed. "And I'll tell you some-

Pictures like this appeared in newspapers and magazines all over the world. Note the peering eyes, the sneer, and the huge, hairy hands.

thing else—he's a mean one, you bet. Remember, he's Gargantua the Great from now on. No more of that 'Buddy' stuff. He's the meanest thing you ever saw. By the way, a man from Burnell's is coming out to make some pictures. Give him whatever help he needs, won't you?"

Roberts and I weren't certain the meeting with the gorilla had not been staged, but if it had, Butler had done a superb job, as usual.

On our walk back to the press car after a stop at the grease joint (lunch stand) for coffee, we saw clusters of visitors making their way through the grounds or watching the elephants at work. Butler led the way, hurrying along and talking about Gargantua.

"We'll make this the meanest monster ever seen on earth, by God!" he promised. "The beast must weigh close to 500 pounds, wouldn't you say? And that thick black fur coat he wears makes him look even bigger. I'll have to check and find out what they feed the big bastard. What a drawing card he'll be!"

Butler called Gargantua "the most terrifying creature ever captured by man." Note the size of his hand and foot in this picture showing him behind bars.

Back in the press car, Braden, probably the best story man the Ringlings ever had, was hammering away on the typewriter. He and Butler already had scraped together all the information they could find on gorillas, and he was turning out press releases.

Butler showed us sketches he was working on. One, outlined in bold, black strokes, had the basics of a jungle scene. He quickly lettered in the words, "Gargantua the Great," on a piece of heavy cardboard and laid it across the bottom of the drawing, then stepped back to appraise his work.

"Been here since eight o'clock," he remarked. "Braden and I've got our hands full with this thing; by God, he's a monster.

"You fellows got everything you need? I've got to put in a call to Gladwyn Hill at the A.P. in New York. If you think of anything else, call us."

On the trip back to town, Ned Roberts and I discussed how we'd handle the story—whether straight news, a feature, or a combination of both. Earl Stumpf would have some ideas, too. We knew chimpanzees were fairly common, but neither of us could recall ever having seen a gorilla.

Butler's idea of adding "the Great" to Gargantua's name may not have been new. There had been "Peter the Great," "Alfred the Great," "Consul the Great," and others among performing chimps, but we agreed it seemed to fit the latest circus attraction very well.

Roland Butler was something of an authority on circus animals, through knowledge gained from trainers and keepers over the years, the last dozen of which he had trumpeted the biggest show of all with such slogans as "The whale among the minnows," and "Loaded with ten thousand wonders from every land."

He had painted golden pictures of such things as performing horses, elephants, lions, tigers, bears, monkeys, birds, and even the giant sea monster called "Goliath."

And he had promoted such exhibits as "Giraffe-neck women from Burma, the greatest educational feature the world has ever known," and "A Tribe of genuine Ubangi savages, with mouths and lips as large as those of full-grown crocodiles! Greatest educational feature of all time! New to civilization from Africa's darkest depths!"

Now, with Gargantua the Great squatting in his cage only a couple of hundred yards away, Butler had the ammunition and imagination to create another "stupendous attraction." It is doubtful, however, that he ever dreamed it would become the best-known and most profitable circus animal of the century.

Gargantua sat calmly for this picture in his cage.

CHAPTER SIX

Normally a Family Man

The gorilla was something of a mystery as recently as thirty-five years ago. His living and mating habits and mental capabilities were as unknown to most Americans as were conditions in his native African habitat.

We did know that all apes are tailless primates and belong to the family Pongidae, and that they include the gorilla, chimpanzee, gibbon, and orang-utan. We considered the chimpanzee the most adaptable and most common, with the gorilla on the other side of the fence—the monster of the African wilds.

Now we know that gorillas normally live and move in families, with a large male as head of the household, which includes younger males, females, and their offspring. They travel by day, searching for food and sunning themselves, and usually sleep in a different location each night in nests built on the ground or in trees.

They are fond of fruit, lettuce, celery, and the wild shallot. In captivity, they also like fruit and vegetables but cultivate a taste for boiled meats such as steak and chicken, and also for chocolate milk, cola drinks, and tea.

The young are considered infants until about the age of two or three. At eight or nine, the male gorilla shows a spurt of growth, much like a boy of ten or twelve, and reaches sexual maturity not long afterward. Their love life is described by those who have studied them in the wild as much like that of humans.

A baby gorilla can be handled like a human infant, and carried with head on shoulder and buttocks supported by the arm, as a mother carries a child. On the other hand, the chimpanzee must be trained to this method of conveyance.

One of Gargantua's favorite foods was bananas, and he would peel them like a human. Note the gaze following every movement of the hand.

Adult male gorillas weigh roughly twice as much as females, but records of any weighing more than 600 pounds are rare, and these are found in zoos, where they are well-fed and often become obese.

The mountain gorilla is considered the aristocrat of the species, and one named Mbongo, in the San Diego Zoo, reportedly weighed in at 602 pounds. His cage mate, Ngagi, tipped 539 pounds.

Mrs. Lintz and Mrs. E. Kenneth Hoyt, of New York and Havana, Cuba, were among the first to raise gorillas in this country. Both these ladies found the ape an interesting pet, and both said they were several steps ahead of the more familiar chimpanzee in mental capacity as well as docility.

Most zoologists today consider gorillas rather harmless creatures, especially when young. Only recently it was reported in the press that a group of scientists had concluded the gorilla is not vicious by nature but is inclined to be gentle, confirming the statement Richard Kroener made about Gargantua thirty-five years ago.

Many trainers say chimpanzees reach their prime as performers at about the age of five, and can be exhibited until they reach ten or twelve. After that, they turn ugly and have to be retired.

On the other hand, at least some gorillas retain their docility to the end. Mlle. Toto, exhibited for many years as Mrs. Gargantua the Great, lived to the age of thirty-six or thirty-eight, and died in the arms of her keeper and friend.

It is surprising that so little was known about gorillas until well into this century. While the chimpanzee was long considered the most intelligent of all wild animals, in a study made in 1922 the gorilla was put at the bottom of the list.

A psychologist who made the study concluded that a gorilla had the mentality of an average eighteen-months old baby. Later findings have proved how wrong he was! But, we didn't know much about the moon and many other things in those days, either.

A report to the Smithsonian Institution in 1936 by Captain C. R. S. Pitman, who spent many months in Africa studying gorillas in their native habitat, quoted an old prospector as saying:

"They do not make much noise, just grunt. I maintain that unless provoked, they are docile. Gorillas sometimes raid gardens but I never heard of them attacking natives, who leave them alone except to chase them from their property."

Captain Pitman also noted the peculiar drumming on the chest and said the partially cupped hands and the way in which they are held, and the way they strike the chest, are responsible for the penetrating nature of the sound.

"It is a wrathful roar, aptly described as a hellish challenge of the angered male," he wrote, "but it is rare. It is a challenge and not necessarily to frighten. They appear to converse in gutteral grunts. The gorilla normally is peaceably disposed and not aggressive."

George B. Schaller, who wrote the definitive book, *The Year of the Gorilla,* in 1964, found that gorillas have good eyesight and hearing, and it compares with that of man. However, their sense of smell is relatively poor.

"When I began to study gorillas," Schaller wrote, "I was tremendously impressed with their human appearance–they gave the superficial impression of slightly retarded persons with rather short legs wrapped in fur coats.

"They yawn when they wake up; stretch, dangle legs, rest with hands behind head, like humans. They frown, bite lips; youngsters go into tantrums. They live like human families, and their mating system is polygamous."

Dian Fossey, who made intensive studies of mountain gorillas at close range in African highlands, wrote of her experiences in the *National Geographic* magazine for January, 1970, and October, 1971.

"A mature male may be six feet tall and weigh 400 pounds or more," Miss Fossey reported. "His enormous arms can span eight feet."

In some 3,000 hours of direct observation and contact, Miss Fossey said, she encountered only a few minutes of what might be called "aggressive behavior."

"These incidents were generally initiated by protective adults when their young approached me too closely," she wrote. "In all instances, the 'charges' proved to be bluff."

Miss Fossey told of an incident involving Peanuts, one of her favorite gorillas encountered during her long study. She extended her hand, and the gorilla, who seemed to ponder accepting it, "came a step closer and, extending his own hand, gently touched his fingers to mine."

It was the first time, to her knowledge, that a wild gorilla ever came so close to holding hands with a human being. Miss Fossey said she was so thrilled and excited she cried.

"The gorilla is one of the most maligned creatures in the world," Miss Fossey concluded, saying she found them to be among the gentlest of animals, and the shiest.

In his entertaining book, *Wild Tigers & Tame Fleas,* Bill Ballantine cited the case of Phil, the gorilla who for years was the star attraction at the St. Louis Zoo.

"Phil is coal black, weighs over 600 pounds, and compared to him Johnny North's highly touted gorilla, the late Gargantua, was a pot-bellied sissy," Ballantine wrote in 1958.

"Phil's head seemed to me as big as a bushel basket; his fingers were as thick as a child's wrist. He romps in a fifty-foot square cage (with swimming pool), and plays with the tire from a twelve-ton truck."

In spite of Phil's size and his impression on Ballantine, the author quoted George Vierheller, the zoo director, as saying "he wouldn't hurt you intentionally."

When he came to the zoo in 1941, Phil reportedly weighed twenty-six pounds and cost three thousand dollars. Vierheller said he would not part with the gorilla for any price, although he suspected Phil was worth more than fifty thousand dollars.

Another authority on primate psychology, Dr. Robert M. Yerkes, concluded that the gorilla is psychologically closer to man than the chimpanzee and seemed to be motivated by more complex factors, choosing to do only that which he wished, or what he found most interesting.

Gorillas and chimpanzees share many structural characteristics with man, including a jointed tail which develops in the embryo, to shrivel later and leave a dimple at the end of the spine.

Gorillas also are prone to many of man's diseases, in captivity. These may include measles, mumps, typhoid fever, cancer, appendicitis, pneumonia, and syphilis. They react to sedatives and stimulants in the same manner as humans.

After eating, Gargantua would sit and pick his teeth. He liked all kinds of fruit, and lived on a rigid diet of the very best meat, whole milk, eggs, cheese, and ice cream.

Gertrude Lintz and Marie Hoyt, with their financial independence, abundant patience, and love of animals, were able to care for their gorillas, treating them like children and studying their habits and characteristics, adding to man's knowledge.

After Buddy joined the circus and became Gargantua the Great, Richard Kroener learned he could not trust the gorilla any more than he could an aging chimp.

"Where have you got that old devil?" Tony Desimone asked Dick during a visit to winter quarters.

"Hush up; don't talk about it," Kroener replied. "Nobody is supposed to know about him yet."

Before his special cage was built, the gorilla was confined in what is known as a deer cage, with bars eight or ten inches apart.

"When I saw that cage," Tony recalls, "I said, 'Dick, somebody's going to feel him. You'd better be careful. He can reach his arms out and get you.' "

A few days later, Gargantua the Great stuck his long arms out through the bars and grabbed the keeper. He lifted Kroener off his feet, pulled him to the cage, and began gnawing on him.

Kroener, alone at the time, happened to have a window hook in his hand and finally managed to whop him on the head and escape. Then he went to the hospital.

"When he had me," Dick said later, "the thought kept going through my head, 'This is it.' "

Animal men kept close watch on Gargantua. Here he is with Frank (Bring 'Em Back Alive) Buck (left) and Richard Kroener, his long-time keeper and companion.

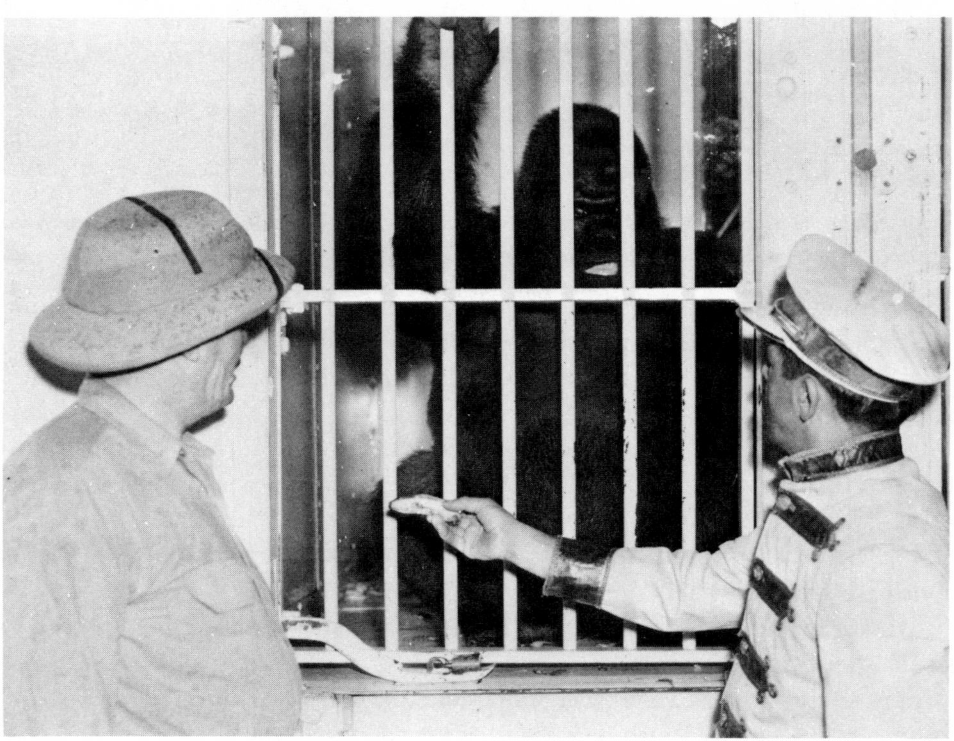

CHAPTER SEVEN

Here Comes Gargantua

Roland Butler knew no more about gorillas when the year 1938 began than the average well-read person. Although he had dealt with circus animals and their handlers in pictures and text for years, his experience with the largest of all primates was extremely limited.

But he was one of the great circus press agents of the century, devoted to extolling the show's many attractions, and a welcome visitor in city rooms throughout America.

When the Ringling Bros. and Barnum & Bailey Combined Shows announced it would feature "Gargantua the Great, the most terrifying creature on earth," the story appeared in newspapers all over the country.

There was a flood of pictures; billboards featured a huge gorilla roaring through the jungle, a native grasped in one hairy hand held high overhead much in the manner of a javelin thrower, all in flaming colors.

Columnists and editorial writers had a field day. Arthur Brisbane, a leading scribe of the time, debated in his widely syndicated column whether the circus gorilla could beat the former world's heavyweight boxing champion, Gene Tunney, who had retired undefeated.

Tunney, a friend of the North brothers, went along with the whimsical reasoning. He was quoted in an interview as saying he could take Gargantua in the first round, with a punch to the solar plexus before the huge ape could bring his greater arm reach and strength into action.

Scientists came to call at winter quarters, and went away shaking their heads, especially if they'd had a chat with Roland Butler. Reporters, photographers, and feature writers streamed in, looking for stories and pictures of the fiendish beast in the fur coat.

"Get him a tire to cut his teeth on; the biggest truck tire you can find," Butler had told the keeper. "We'll have pictures."

Advertisements featured Gargantua twisting a tire into the figure eight. He was pictured in every conceivable pose calculated to stir the imagination and draw crowds to his cage.

All that winter Gargantua lived in a cage parked inside a tent. One day it was reported that John Ringling North, the new circus president, was walking past when the gorilla flicked out a hand, pulled him to the bars, and took a king-size bite out of the circus man's arm.

The story made headlines across the country, of course. Butler, ever alert to any news possibility, followed it with a press release saying the new circus president had been given "The most massive anti-tetanus shot ever administered to a human being."

Dr. J. Y. Henderson, the show's veterinarian for many years, who wrote the book, *Circus Doctor,* with Richard Taplinger in 1951, had this to say about the incident and the Kroener attack.

"Once Gargantua nearly killed Kroener when he walked too close to his cage, and another time Gargantua grabbed John Ringling North by both sleeves of a leather jacket.

"If North hadn't been strong enough to tear himself out of that jacket, and leave the sleeves dangling in Gargantua's hands, there would probably be another director of the Ringling Circus today."

North had won the position through the cooperation of his aunt, Mrs. Edith Ringling, and his cousin by marriage, Mrs. Aubrey Ringling, both substantial shareholders, in one of the many shifts in management that followed the death of John Ringling in 1936. Henry Ringling North became vice president and assistant to the president.

With spring coming on and time approaching for the circus to leave on its annual tour, North began to think more and more about keeping the big ape alive. He knew that gorillas normally live in tropical jungles, away from disease-carrying humans. He also knew that Gargantua was susceptible to many human ills, particularly those of the respiratory system.

Exposed to circus crowds, he might catch anything. And he was exposed, even in winter quarters, where hundreds visited him daily and pressed close to the cage to have a better look. No efforts were made to hide him now that word was out.

One of Gargantua's favorite playthings was an automobile tire. It was chained to the ceiling and he could swing on it or twist it into the shape of a pretzel.

When he wanted to relax, Gargantua could flop down on his steel table. Note the automobile tire lying on the floor where he left it.

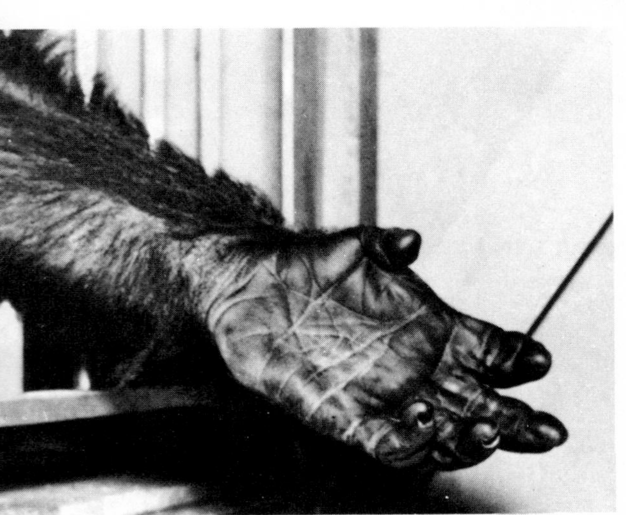

Palmists would have had a field day studying the wrinkles in Gargantua's massive hand, which would have fit into a size 11 glove.

Gargantua, only seven and one-half inches over five feet tall, had an arm reach of nine feet as shown in this rare photograph in his cage, which he never left.

Tony Desimone recalls that Gargantua liked watermelon, and after eating the meat, he would fling the rinds at his visitors.

Roscoe Frey, long-time *Tampa Tribune* photographer who made many pictures of the great ape, recalls that Gargantua could be rather rude at times. While crowds stood gawking in silent curiosity, he would urinate in his cupped hands, and toss it out onto the scattering humans!

North telephoned Lemuel Bulware at the Carrier Corporation in Syracuse, New York, at four o'clock one morning—a normal hour for him to call—and proposed that Carrier build the air-conditioned cage for his gorilla.

Bulware didn't appreciate the hour, but North was quick to point out that the project would bring considerable publicity to the builder as well as the circus.

The result was a glass and steel prison on wheels, designed by Mrs. Lintz, to protect Gargantua from the weather and crowds, and the crowds from him.

The main room was twenty feet long by seven wide, with a smaller sleeping compartment that extended the overall length to twenty-six feet. Hard steel bars were set close together, and the cage was enclosed in two thicknesses of glass, with air space between. The ends were made of three-eighths-inch thick steel plate, and the cage had an oak floor.

It came equipped with thermostatic controls and humidifiers to keep the temperature at seventy-six degrees, humidity fifty percent.

Inside, a swing was suspended by heavy link chain and there was Butler's tire, which Gargantua used as a plaything much like a boy rolls and tosses a hoop.

William Yeske, who had built circus wagons for the Ringlings for forty years, put together a magnificent cage wagon for the star, and Carrier Corporation used the phrase "jungle-conditioned cage" to win the Advertisers' Award for the year.

With Butler, Braden, and the rest of the press corps turning out reams of copy and batches of photographs, Gargantua the Great quickly became a box office sensation.

"Mightiest monster ever captured by man!" screamed one large, multi-colored poster. "Most fiendishly ferocious brute that breathes!" said another. "The world's most terrifying living creature!" and "Largest gorilla ever exhibited alive!"

The circus magazine and review sold at every performance had this to say about the great ape:

"Generally conceded to be an educational feature without equal in all history, Gargantua the Great, now being exhibited for the first time by the Ringling Bros. and Barnum & Bailey Combined Shows, is the largest and most ferocious gorilla ever brought before the eyes of civilized man.

"Weighing a quarter of a ton, and declared by outstanding authorities to possess the muscular power of twenty-seven men, the tremendous strength of this extraordinary primate is overshadowed only by the demoniacal ferocity of his appearance.

"Gargantua the Great is the only full-grown gorilla ever seen on this continent. He was captured by natives of the coastal region of the Belgian Congo, and brought to America by a sea captain.

"From within an air-conditioned and specially-constructed steel-barred and shatter-proof glass enclosed cage, Gargantua the Great glares at patrons of The Greatest Show on Earth who, thanks to the cell-block construction of his prison, may gaze at this fearsome primate without possibility of danger."

Two pictures of the gorilla appeared in the publication. One was entitled "Portrait of Gargantua the Great," and the other showed his hand with left forefinger pointing to the spot on a globe where he was born. It was labeled "Striking contrast," and the cut-lines read:

"The massive hand of Gargantua the Great and that of a normal sized man emphasizes the almost unbelievable concentrated power behind the giant gorilla's forefinger, which points to his approximate place of origin in the dim forests of western equatorial Africa."

Henry Ringling North, who with Alden Hatch wrote the book, *The Circus Kings,* cited interesting incidents to describe Gargantua's mental capabilities.

Curators reported that Gargantua's foot, seen here in center of picture, would have filled a size 12 DDDD shoe.

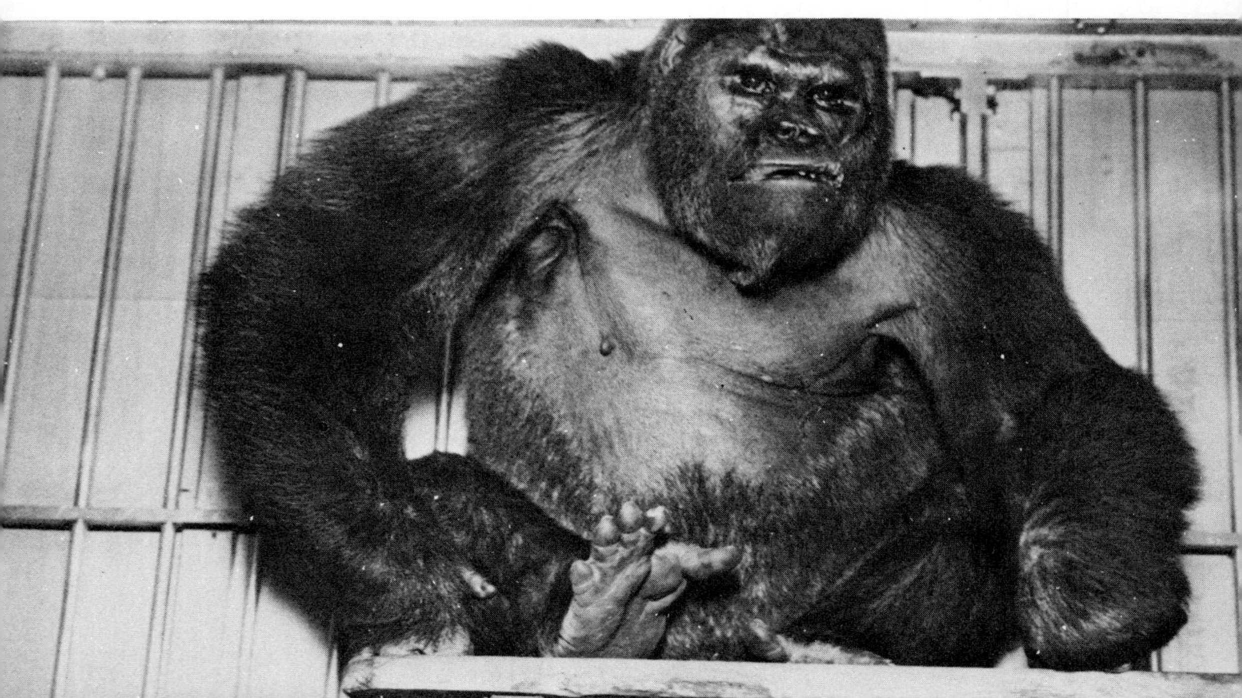

With this frightening expression, Gargantua would have been a formidable foe as a football tackle or guard, with quick reflexes and tremendous strength.

North pointed out that anthropologists disagree on the ape's mental capacity, and added that, "In comparison with the chimpanzee, I vote for the gorilla." He said Gargantua "Was doubtless a thinking character," and compared his mentality with that of a maliciously mischievous moron.

North reported that the gorilla liked to play catch, and they always used a softball. When the ball was thrown into the cage, Gargantua would catch it and throw it back, underhand. Then, suddenly, he would switch from toss to throw, and fling the ball at his partner's head like a baseball pitcher throwing his high, hard one.

Gargantua also liked to play tug of war, North recalled. When the end of a rope was thrown into his cage, he would pull it, sometimes letting the human win.

"But he could always win if he wanted to," North added. "Each time the

Some said Gargantua had a snarl, but it was a sneer, defined as "A scornful facial expression characterized by a slight raising of one corner of the upper lip."

gorilla threw the end of the rope out, he would shorten it, hoping thus to lure the human player closer so he could grab or bite."

Writing about Gargantua in his book, *Center Ring,* Robert Lewis Taylor paid tribute to his great drawing power and said the gorilla was "As popular as [Bing] Crosby, and as temperamental as [Greta] Garbo."

Experts in box office ratings, Taylor reported, "feel that Gargantua is as well known as any performer in the country."

In one 25-day stand in Madison Square Garden, the circus took in $650,000, much of it attributable to Gargantua's tremendous public appeal.

He drew more paying customers to the circus than P. T. Barnum's Jumbo. However, it may be noted that the big elephant trouped only four seasons, from 1882 through 1885, when the population was fairly sparse compared to the late 1930s and 1940s of Gargantua. Also, in Jumbo's day, transportation was limited to trains, boats, streetcars, bicycles, and horse and carriage.

When Gargantua came along, the automobile was commonplace, and so was the airplane. The circus could and often did draw 10,000 or more for a single performance. With the ape as a feature attraction, the Ringling Bros. and Barnum & Bailey Combined Shows often took in well over $50,000 a day for two performances, well over twice the cost of operation.

It has not done as well since.

CHAPTER EIGHT

He's Worth $100,000

Father Elslander of the Episcopal Church blessed the trains as usual when the circus left winter quarters on April Fool's Day in 1938 for the opening in New York's Madison Square Garden a week later.

The four trains were made up of ninety cars of flats, freights, and coaches jammed with circus personnel and equipment—cookhouse stoves, pots, pans, and dishes; canvas, poles, lines, seats; trucks, buses, wagons; props, costumes; ring stock, elephants, horses, camels, zebras, and all the hundreds of other animals and birds.

Gargantua the Great's glittering cage was on one of the long, silver-sided flats, covered with canvas. Inside was the new star the public was waiting to see.

When the show opened on April 8 for a three week stand, the gorilla was a sensation. Capacity crowds filled the Garden for every performance, but there was trouble ahead.

Four nights later, workingmen struck for higher wages. What happened was that Sam Gumpertz, who'd taken over as executive vice president and general manager when John Ringling defaulted on his notes in 1932, had run the show during the worst days of the Depression, sometimes on borrowed money.

He had signed a contract with the American Federation of Actors, an American Federation of Labor affiliate, representing the workingmen or roustabouts. It was for five years and was still in force when John Ringling North took over in that spring of 1938.

The pay scale that prevailed in winter quarters held over in New York and Boston, or until the show went under canvas. Then the minimum wage was to be doubled.

A union delegation called on North and demanded that the higher pay scale go into effect immediately. North in effect told them to "go to hell," and vowed that the show would go on. Everybody except staff members, performers, and sideshow personnel walked out.

North had hired Charles LeMaire, a Broadway showman, to create a pageant featuring Gargantua the Great, with Frank (Bring 'Em Back Alive) Buck as the Maharajah of Nepal. This feature alone reportedly cost $80,000.

Biggest problem the first night of the strike was getting Gargantua to the show, moving his cumbersome cage up the runway and into the arena. Normally, this required six draft horses, a skilled driver, and his helpers. On this night there were none.

A chugging little tractor couldn't do the job, and for a time it appeared the star wouldn't make it. But fifty eager volunteers crowded around, among them a sprinkling of circus officials and their guests, in dress suits; several performers, and a sizable crowd from the audience.

They shoved, pulled, and pushed the glittering cage up the runway and into the arena, picking up more pushers as the procession moved along the hippodrome track.

There were so many people swarming around the cage that spectators in the seats couldn't get even a glimpse of Gargantua. However, they were almost as interested in the big glass and steel compartment as they were in the gorilla himself.

In his book, *The Big Top,* with Hartzell Spence, Fred Bradna, long-time circus equestrian director, told of an incident about that time when three inquisitive newsmen came calling.

Gargantua's cage was appropriately decorated to resemble a jungle scene, but the bars were of hard steel. Dual wheels were essential to support and move the stout prison cell.

Bradna said Lucius Beebe, Harry Staton and Geoffrey Parsons wanted to inspect the cage close up. Gargantua was in the living section, and Parsons opened the door to the smaller sleeping quarters for a look inside. As Beebe poked his head in to test the air-conditioning, Parsons and Staton shoved him inside and slammed the door.

"At that moment," said Bradna, "the whistle blew for Gargantua to make his appearance and tour the arena. Spectators were puzzled to see a man, huddled to escape recognition, riding in air-conditioned discomfort in Gargantua's display case."

The labor problem was solved briefly, and the Madison Square Garden engagement lasted through April 30 in 1938. The circus moved on to Boston for a stand in the Garden there from May 2 through 7, and escaped labor difficulties until it reached Brooklyn on May 9.

Organized labor began boycotting the show, and there were some scattered incidents during five days in Brooklyn and two in Washington, D.C. The problem multiplied in Baltimore, Philadelphia, Newark, Trenton, and Wilmington.

The show moved on to Reading, Harrisburg, and Pittsburgh; it canceled a Cleveland date and played Wheeling, West Virginia, before going to Columbus, Dayton, Lima, and Sandusky.

One-day stands took it to Fort Wayne, Toledo, Erie, and then into upstate New York, where business was no better. The circus was really hurting when it limped out of Binghampton on the night of June 21, and headed for Scranton, Pennsylvania.

The next afternoon, when Bradna blew his whistle for the performance to start, workingmen struck again. In this labor-conscious city, the great amusement enterprise lay helpless for two days and nights, much of the time without food or water.

Finally, nonstriking personnel loaded the trains and headed for winter quarters in Florida, the first time the big show was forced to close in mid-season.

In January, 1938, I went to work for the United Press in its Atlanta bureau, and from there kept abreast of circus happenings by telephone, telegram, and letter, later going to Sarasota for the climax.

The Ringling combine also included the Al G. Barnes and Sells-Floto Circus, which at that time was playing the Midwest. Outstanding features from the Ringling show and a trainload of physical equipment left winter quarters, with Henry Ringling North in charge, to join the smaller unit at Redfield, South Dakota, on July 11. The billing matter read:

"Al G. Barnes and Sells-Floto Circus, presenting Ringling Bros. and Barnum & Bailey Stupendous New Features."

The program included Mabel Stark, the noted wild animal trainer hailed as "The Queen of the Jungle, presenting a notable congress of the earth's most ferocious performing lions and tigers."

It also offered such attractions as a lion riding a horse, several flying acts, clowns, Roman chariot races, and, of course, Gargantua the Great.

It was the first season with John Ringling North and his brother, Henry, at the helm, and it very well may have been the last if it hadn't been for Gargantua's tremendous drawing power.

Thousands of people in North and South Dakota, and in nineteen other states in the Midwest and South, were anxious to see what the circus proclaimed was "The mightiest monster ever captured by man!" Some couldn't even pronounce his name, but they knew what they'd come to see.

Merle Evans, who led the circus band from 1919 through 1969, remembers one time when he came out of the Big Top after a performance in the deep South, and met a party of Negroes trying to find their way to the gorilla's cage.

"Where's that thing they call 'Guarantee'?" one of them asked the band leader, who directed them to the menagerie tent.

The 1938 tour lasted until November 27, when the circus rolled into Sarasota, gave afternoon and evening performances for the "home folks," and went into winter quarters.

It marked the end of the Al G. Barnes and Sells-Floto circus, but in little more than four months these old and respected names in the outdoor entertainment world, featuring Gargantua the Great, produced enough revenue for John Ringling North to report a profit of $400,000 for the season instead of $40,000 a week he claimed the show was losing when it reached Scranton.

North immediately began planning for the 1939 season, starting with a new Big Top, oval-shaped and with four instead of the usual six center poles. He had plans for other innovations, too.

"Let's make the canvas blue," he said, and blue it was—dark blue at the peak, shading to light blue at the base, with center poles painted gold and quarter poles silver. Gold stars glittered in the center-of-the-ring carpets and on all poles and drapes.

It was impossible to air-condition a circus tent of that size, but the Norths did the next best thing. They put in giant blowers to fetch in cold air, and the patrons liked it, especially during midsummer matinees. The North brothers were proving themselves extremely capable showmen.

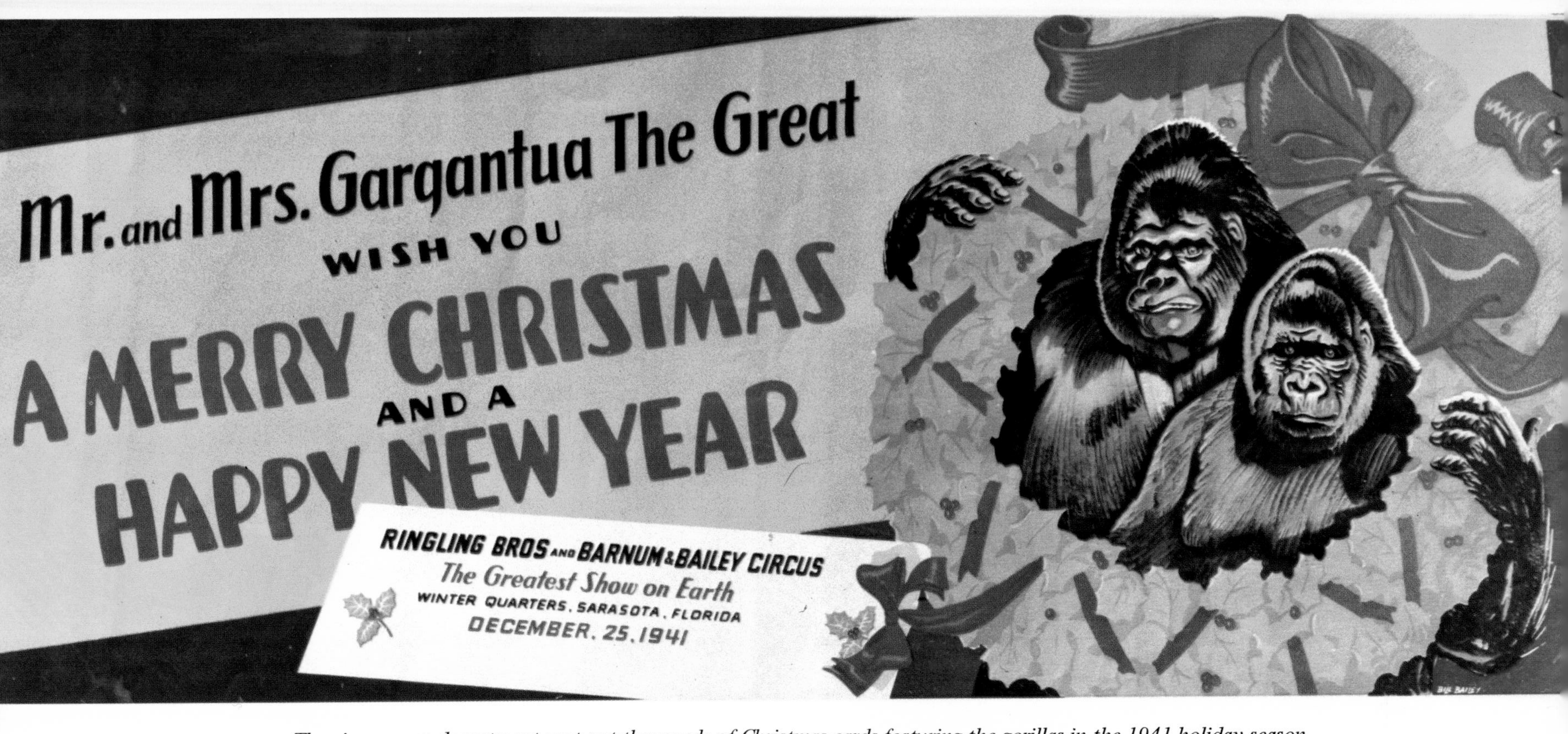

Mr. and Mrs. Gargantua The Great
WISH YOU
A MERRY CHRISTMAS
AND A
HAPPY NEW YEAR
RINGLING BROS AND BARNUM & BAILEY CIRCUS
The Greatest Show on Earth
WINTER QUARTERS, SARASOTA, FLORIDA
DECEMBER. 25, 1941

The circus press department sent out thousands of Christmas cards featuring the gorillas in the 1941 holiday season.

During World War II, Gargantua and M' Toto promoted the sale of war bonds, and government officials praised them for their war effort. This was one of the posters displayed.

During the 1939 season, circus officials reported, they took in $650,000 during the Madison Square Garden engagement alone, from April 5 through 29, and $2,635,000 for the tour that took the show into Canada, Washington, Oregon and California, Texas, and finally Florida, ending the season on October 30 in Tampa.

A major portion of the circus' revenue in the 1938 and 1939 seasons came from Gargantua the Great. Thousands swarmed to his cage to peer in, happy to buy picture postcards and programs featuring the famous gorilla. Sales of pictures, folders, and the circus magazine were always brisk.

The public had a continuing appetite for facts about Gargantua, and he was featured in countless newspaper and magazine stories.

Earl J. Johnson, at that time vice president and news director of United Press, interviewed John Ringling North during a visit to Sarasota and asked the circus man, point blank, "How much did you pay for Gargantua?"

Other newsmen, including the writer, had tried to unearth this bit of information many times from various sources, but it was a closely guarded secret.

North hesitated a moment or two, turning his hazel eyes and Irish smile from one to another of us awaiting his reply. Then he looked directly at the news executive from New York and said, "He's worth a hundred thousand dollars."

It probably was the only time in history that a circus man made such a conservative claim. Surely it was the understatement of the week!

CHAPTER NINE

The Wedding

Johnny North, the thirty-six-year-old circus impressario and promoter, not only was busy running the show, with the able assistance of his younger brother, Henry, but he was an executor of his Uncle John's sprawling estate, and that was giving him headaches.

The late circus king had willed that his only sister, Ida Ringling North, and her son, John, were to be executors of his estate, but in a codicil he cut her inheritance to $5,000 a year, and made it clear his nephew wasn't to inherit a dime.

Ringling's holdings included hotels, beach property, ranchlands, railroads, oil wells, a bank, and several circuses. The job of bringing order out of this chaos was enough to keep three men busy, and one had to have been brought up in this volatile and frequently feuding family to be able to untangle the twenty million dollar mess.

In that fall of 1939, when the circus was settled in winter quarters, North devoted some time to trying to settle the estate, including having appraisals made of paintings in the John and Mable Ringling Museum of Art. Three appraisers fixed the value of the museum and its contents at twelve million dollars.

North went to Europe for what turned out to be a pleasant and profitable journey. He sent Gargantua the Great and his keeper, Kroener, to London by freighter from New Orleans to fill an engagement with the Bertram Mills Circus at the Olympia. The gorilla proved to be a sensational attraction.

When North returned to Florida, he brought along minutes of a meeting of the Rembrandt Corporation, where he was elected president and his brother secretary-treasurer.

This was one of those things John Ringling had set up with himself as president; his wife, Mable, and Julius Boehler, an art connoisseur and friend, as incorporators for the museum and contents. In the minutes, no mention was made of Boehler, only member of the incorporating trio still alive.

Incidentally, the museum was the most valuable piece of property in John Ringling's estate, which was not settled until 1946. His total holdings were appraised at $22,366,000.

Meanwhile, Gargantua the Great thrived in his antiseptic cage under the watchful eye of Richard Kroener, who saw that he had everything a gorilla might wish for, except freedom.

Gargantua bounded about the cage, playing with his big tire and swing enough to keep his muscles in tone. He was not becoming obese, nor even putting on weight as fast as the press agents hoped, although he was fed morning, noon, and night, with tea in the afternoon.

Regardless of how much Gargantua's cousins might have scrounged in the wilds of Africa, they couldn't have matched his vittles in the air-conditioned cage. He ate nothing but the best and most tasty.

The 1940 season was a good one, beginning in Madison Square Garden on April 5, moving to Boston May 2, then going under canvas at Baltimore on May 13. The tour carried the circus north to Maine, west to the Dakotas and Nebraska, south to Texas, and back to the Atlantic coast before the season ended at Sarasota on November 18.

There had been no serious labor trouble, no fires, no heavy storms to cause blowdown, or other misfortunes, and the show played 148 cities in 37 states that season.

But in Europe fighting was increasing, and America was being drawn closer and closer to World War II. There were many more things to think about besides circuses, including jobs in defense plants, plus rationing of tires and gasoline.

The Norths sensed that Gargantua the Great might lose some of his appeal in the 1941 season. After all, their press department had exhausted its supply of superlatives. It was time to come up with something new. On the circus' back yard, Gargantua already had been nicknamed "Gargy," indicating a touch of affection or at least familiarity. That would never do. It was time to come up with something new.

They had learned of a female gorilla then living in Havana, Cuba, and North correctly reasoned that this would be a worthwhile addition to the circus. He went to Havana to negotiate in person with the gorilla's owner, Mrs. E. Kenneth Hoyt.

Meanwhile, in Havana there lived Mrs. Marie Hoyt and her pet, a gorilla named Mademoiselle Toto, about the same age as Gargantua.

Marie Hoyt and her late husband had been given the nine-pound baby gorilla by a chieftain in the French Congo, who explained it was "too small to eat." The time was February, 1932, and they named the infant "Toto," which in Swahili means "baby."

After a stop in Paris, the Hoyts returned to their New York home, taking along the gorilla. After Hoyt died, his widow went to Havana, where she bought a mansion on the outskirts of the city.

Mrs. Hoyt hired a keeper named Jose Tomas, who had migrated from his native Barcelona, Spain, to Cuba, and worked at the primate colony owned by Madame Rosalia Abreu. Tomas married a pretty Cuban girl named Emilia.

The wealthy Mrs. Hoyt built a separate house for Toto on her estate, and the gorilla lived happily in the salubrious climate of Cuba. She and Tomas got along famously.

Like Mrs. Lintz, Mrs. Hoyt had a motherly attachment for her gorilla, ate lunch with it every day, and they had tea in the garden at three o'clock every afternoon. Tomas loved Toto and was her constant companion. They played much as a brother and sister would, making letters with pencils, painting, and playing chess. He carried Toto on his back, and rode on hers.

Mrs. Hoyt would never think of selling her pet, although press reports at the time said North paid the same for her as he did for Gargantua.

What happened was they reached a lease agreement whereby Toto would

Mademoiselle Toto had a happy home life with a swing and a patient, experienced keeper named Jose Tomas from Barcelona, Spain.

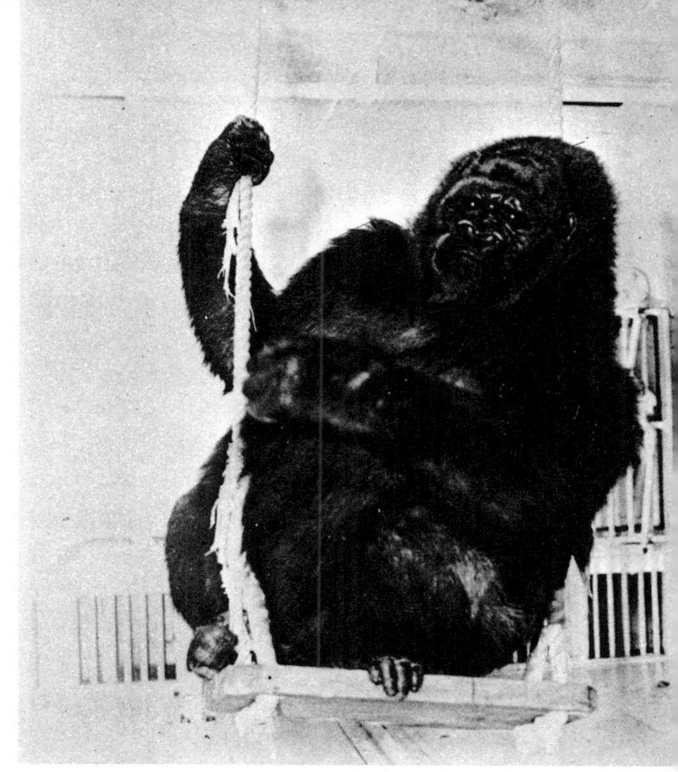

Jose Tomas played with Toto every day, and taught her to ride on his back. At this time he said she weighed over 400 pounds.

be exhibited in a glass and steel air-conditioned cage exactly like Gargantua's, with Tomas as her keeper. Mrs. Hoyt retained possession, and was allowed to visit Toto any hour of the day or night.

Tomas and Toto arrived in this country the middle of February, 1941, by ship at Port Everglades, the port for Fort Lauderdale, Florida. By coincidence, the United Press had transferred me to Miami from Birmingham early in December, 1940.

Jack Frankish, U.P. bureau manager at Miami, assigned me and Mike Ackerman, the veteran photographer for Acme Newspapers, to cover the gorilla's arrival. The circus had kept all news sources advised, of course, and a score of reporters and photographers gathered at the dock to meet Tomas and the latest circus attraction, now being referred to as Mlle. Toto or M'Toto.

Paul Danovsky, a Ringling employee for many years, had taken the cage from winter quarters to Havana. Danovsky, Tomas, and Toto made the cross-country journey from Fort Lauderdale to Sarasota by train. We drove to Sarasota with Ackerman and his trusty old speed graphic camera.

In winter quarters, circus officials, including the press agents, greeted the new arrival and immediately announced plans for a "gorilla wedding." Of course, they emphasized, it would be "The first in the history of the world."

This earth-shaking event was scheduled for Washington's birthday, February 22. The date fit nicely between the time of Mlle. Toto's arrival and the circus' departure on tour. Also, the publicity department wisely reasoned that it would get far better newspaper and radio coverage on a national holiday, when most business houses were closed and spot news was limited.

Mrs. Hoyt, an attractive, lively, and very warm person, was strongly opposed to any sort of so-called wedding between her pet and Gargantua the Great at that time. She told circus officials dear Toto was exhausted and upset after the long trip from Havana, and in no condition to go through with such an exciting experience.

"I am opposed to any wedding," she said, emphasizing the last word. "My baby needs rest and privacy."

However, the stage was set. Scores of writers and photographers had descended upon winter quarters from all parts of the country; still and motion picture cameras were being set up and checked out.

On the morning of the wedding, Roland Butler assured restless newsmen

Meanwhile, Gargantua the Great sat in his cage, doing absolutely nothing. Circus officials thought it would be a capital idea to find the gorilla a "bride."

that it would go on as planned, but would be moved up an hour, to two-thirty o'clock.

Word had spread through the town, and an unusually large number of visitors showed up, even for a holiday. They used every conceivable excuse to get into the tent where the ceremony was to take place. The crush was so great that Butler and his aides had trouble finding working room for the press.

Mrs. Hoyt, who still frowned on the idea, apparently had not been told of the change in the hour. She had gone into town on an errand; it would be wise to get this thing over before she returned.

Quickly, a tractor was hooked onto Mlle. Toto's cage, and it was wheeled into the managerie tent, a spread big enough to accommodate both gorilla cages and a couple of hundred people.

On the side of the cage was a sign, for the benefit of photographers, reading: "Mrs. Gargantua the Great." On the other enclosure was a hand-lettered sign, heavy black on white cardboard. It read: "Gargantua the Great."

Tomas, the keeper, was watching his pet closely, but he could not stop the wedding. Neither could Kroener, who paced nervously along the side of "Gargy's" cage, frequently being interrupted to have his picture taken.

Mlle. Toto sat in a corner of her cage, curiously eyeing every move. Gargantua paced the floor, hopping into and out of his swing; bounding to a corner to grasp his tire, flinging it against the side of his cage, or rolling it across the floor, and stopping frequently to peer at the crowd.

In the business office nearby, someone put on a record and turned up the volume so Lohengrin's "Processional" could be heard all over winter quarters and onto the Bobby Jones golf course adjoining.

The crowd pressed closer as the chattering tractor backed and pushed Mlle. Toto's cage into place. Workingmen removed the end pieces, leaving only bars. Gargantua's compartment was closed, but the panels were quickly slid out, and the two cages bumped end to end.

For a moment, both gorillas stared in stunned curiosity. The tent was filled with a church-like stillness; people and animals stood like so many statues in a museum.

Then Gargantua the Great reached for a stalk of celery held by his keeper, turned, and shoved it through the bars, a gift for the bride.

This is Gargantua at the time of the "wedding," on February 22, 1941. Roland Butler, the press agent, would have called it a fine study of the meanest monster on earth.

Mlle. Toto stared disdainfully, then moved closer, but they did not touch. She seemed overwhelmed with cautious curiosity, or perhaps perplexity. Tomas remained discreetly in the background.

Mlle. Toto inched toward Gargantua, then with a lightninglike thrust of a furry hand, knocked the offering loose. It fell to the floor with a loud "splat." She quickly picked it up and flung it back into his cage.

The big gorilla, with a puzzled look on his face, next offered a few lettuce leaves, but Mlle. Toto wanted no part of those, either. She looked quizzically at him, turned, bounded to the far end of her cage, and sat down!

At that instant, Mrs. Hoyt returned. She pushed her way through the crowd, muttering in obvious disapproval. She carried a large bouquet of flowers and a box of candy. She poked the bouquet through the bars, and her gorilla accepted them with what could only be described as appreciation.

The crowd broke into applause, and Mrs. Hoyt managed a faint smile. The gorillas showed complete disinterest in each other, and made no further attempts to approach or communicate. Neither made a sound.

The "wedding" turned out differently from that of Bamboo and Massa in the Philadelphia Zoo more than five years earlier. Writing about it in the zoo's publication of December, 1966, Frederick A. Ulmer, Jr., the curator of mammals, had this to say:

"Placed in a cage next to Bamboo, the newcomer (Massa) 'coquettishly beat her chest with her strong hairy hands after tossing a few straws into Bamboo's cage,' according to newsmen present.

"Bamboo, meanwhile, would rush across his cage in one of his shuffling charges. As events later proved, the two gorillas were trying to intimidate each other."

Zoo officials learned soon after Massa's arrival that both were males. They put a special doorway between their two cages so that if Bamboo got too rough, Massa could retreat through the small opening, without Bamboo following.

"In all, the gorillas engaged in some seven tussles," Ulmer reported, "and after about two hours, each retired to a neutral corner to catch his breath. Most observers gave the younger Massa the decision."

The "wedding" of Gargantua the Great and Mlle. Toto ended as quickly and quietly as it began. When one reporter made a dash for the nearest telephone, others charged after him, to write or dictate their stories.

The bride, Mademoiselle Toto, on her arrival in Florida for the "wedding" with Gargantua which never came off. Anyway, she was billed as Madame Toto or M' Toto and as Mrs. Gargantua the Great.

The crowd dispersed. Within five minutes, only the keepers, Mrs. Hoyt, a few circus hands, and half a dozen inquiring individuals remained. The "wedding" had been a decided flop from a news standpoint, and particularly for pictures.

The bridal couple remained in their respective compartments through that night and thereafter. But the circus press agents had a new and exciting gem with which to work. They made the most of it.

The two gorilla cages were parked end-to-end but circus officials concluded Gargantua was too strong and dangerous to be turned loose with M' Toto.

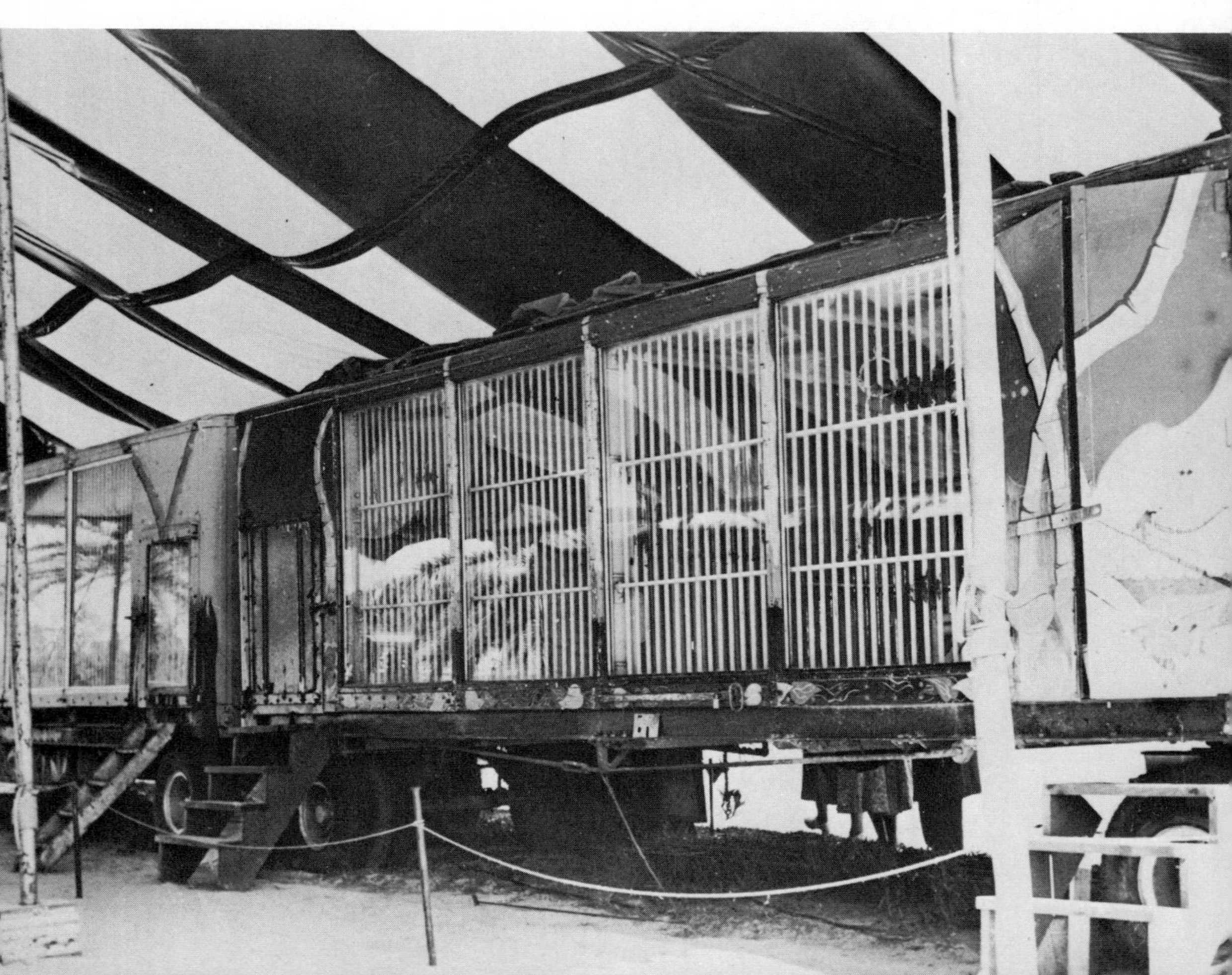

CHAPTER TEN

Life with Mr. and Mrs. Gargantua

After their wedding, circus press agents did a superb job of promoting the gorillas and keeping the attraction alive. They were billed as "Mr. and Mrs. Gargantua the Great, the only gorilla couple in captivity, living happily in air-conditioned comfort."

The press department prepared an attractive brochure, stating many facts and fancies about the "newly-married gorillas," quoting the keepers as saying, "Gargantua loves Toto," and "Toto loves Gargantua."

The literature quoted Kroener and Tomas as saying, "I've got a real love match on my hands," and made other pronouncements aimed at keeping the public interested in the lives of the apes.

At first the two keepers were mystified, but they were real troupers and went along, never denying a single statement the press agents attributed to them.

In their situation, it was a simple matter to ignore or evade probing questions from newsmen and the public. Kroener spoke English very well but could always lapse into his native German, and leave inquiring towners gaping. Tomas still speaks very little English, so he could look puzzled, and reply in all truth, "No speak English."

Either Kroener or Tomas was at the cages around the clock, carefully guarding their charges, watching their well-being, and catering to their every need and whimsy.

Mrs. Hoyt was there every day, keeping a motherly eye on her "baby," seeing to it that she had the best food and attention, giving her tidbits of candy and other goodies.

Mrs. Lintz visited occasionally, but it was not convenient for her to make these sentimental journeys often. In her book, *Animals Are My Hobby,* she wrote that "I went to see Buddy as often as possible, to keep a little rift open through the darkness that covers his world.

"As long as I can go to the back of the cage so that I can reach him through the bars, and hug his great grotesque body, and put my fingers inside his mouth to see how his second teeth are coming on, so long Buddy knows there is one person who does not consider him a brute beast and killer."

Over the entrance to the tent where the gorillas were exhibited when the circus was on tour was this sign, in flaming letters:

"Gorilla Land, Featuring Mr. and Mrs. Gargantua the Great, only gorilla couple in captivity."

Neither did anything to thrill or entertain the customers, but both could be seen through the thick glass, and that was enough to draw hordes of people day after day in cities across the nation—to pay admission, stand and stare, ask questions, and buy picture postcards and other literature.

Gargantua the Great and Mme. Toto ate the same food at the same time each day. They were fed three times daily, and had warm tea at three o'clock in the afternoon, with a little whiskey. Both were fond of tea.

Here is the complete daily menu, with feeding instructions:

Breakfast

8:00 a.m. 1 1/2 quarts of milk mixed with Ovaltine or other malt
3 jelly sandwiches
ALL MILK AND TEA AND OTHER FOODS ARE TO BE SWEETENED WITH DARK BROWN SUGAR ONLY.

Dinner

11:00 a.m.	8 bananas	*Occasional tidbits*
	5 oranges	peanuts
	1 pear	apple pie
	1 apple	canned peaches
	1/2 lb. of grapes	canned pineapple
	1 tomato	ice cream
	1/2 head of lettuce	custard pie
	1 corn on the cob	cream cheese
	2 slices of American cheese	

One time a week he is to get a 1 to 1 1/2 lb. steak broiled or fried RARE.

One time a week he is to get one whole broiled chicken

Two times a week he is to get rice mixed with 3 soft-boiled eggs
Three times a week he is to get pea soup mixed half-and-half with water with 3 soft-boiled eggs mixed in

3:00 p.m. 1 1/2 quarts of warm tea with a shot of whiskey sweetened with dark brown sugar

Supper

6:00 p.m. 1 1/2 quarts of warm milk mixed with Ovaltine or Cocoa Malt
3 jelly sandwiches
Feeding instructions also included these notations:
If the bananas are a little dry and he won't eat them, mash them up and mix them with canned peaches.
If he does not eat his oranges, save them and give him orange juice.

The gorillas liked steak and chicken, and if they were given more than the allotted portions, they would not eat their vegetables or dessert.

They would take the broiled chicken, carefully pick off the meat, and throw out the bones. They would peel bananas and oranges with their fingers, just like humans. Keepers reported both were fond of Coca-Cola.

Richard Kroener died of cancer in 1942, and Tomas took over as head keeper, his title being "Superintendent of the gorillas." His assistants, at various times, included Harry Albert, Joseph A. Madieros, Martha G. Hunter, Peter J. Clare, Raymond Simpson, John Corricelli, and Alex Nelson.

The stocky, graying Tomas now lives in happy retirement in a luxurious home on the outskirts of Sarasota, with his charming wife, Emilia. Their three sons–Joseph, Kenneth and Robert–are grown and out on their own.

Tomas thumbs through a thick album of pictures and clippings, fondly

(left) *What's this, fleas? M' Toto had plenty of time to keep her pet kitten free of fleas, as shown here.* (middle) *The kitten often perched on M' Toto's back while the gorilla lolled in her swing.* (right) *Toto had plenty to amuse and entertain herself, including this black and white kitten.*

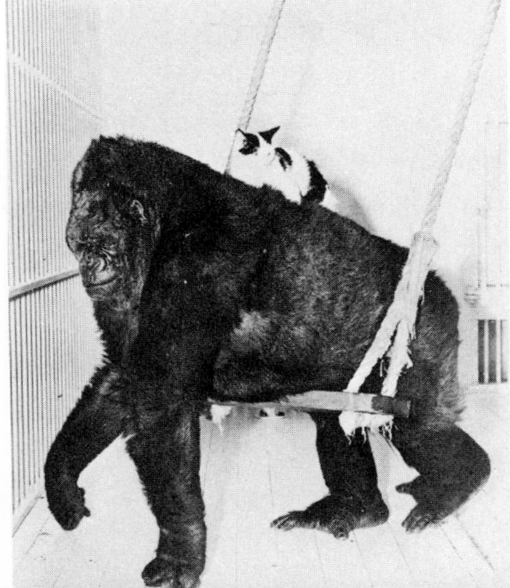

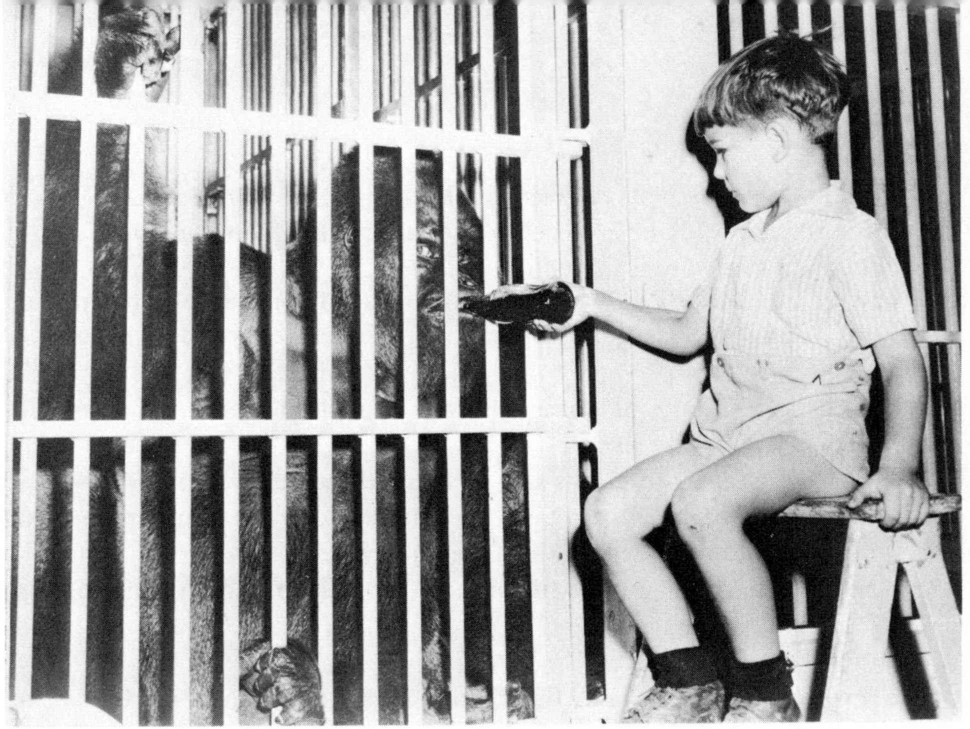

Kenneth Tomas, son of Toto's keeper, gives Gargantua a bottle of his favorite soft drink.

recalling his life with Toto in Cuba during the good years, and with the circus afterward.

There are pictures of Toto perched on her keeper's back, piggyback style; of Tomas riding her with legs draped over her powerful shoulders; of them playing chess, checkers, and other games.

"Toto always gentle," Tomas recalls in his delightful Spanish accent. "The female always more gentle than male. Toto never caged in Cuba, never; loose all time. She play with cats, dogs—anything.

"I taught her count on fingers and toes. She do anything! She throw me kisses. She loved people look at her. Gargantua never like people."

Tomas declared that Toto never harmed her keeper, nor Mrs. Hoyt; that she was gentle to the end of her life, and never ill.

He denied he ever bathed Toto, as some claimed, but rubbed her body with cod liver oil, a foul-smelling substance full of vitamins A and D. This confirms what other gorilla men have said—the big apes do not particularly like water on their bodies. They give off an acrid body odor, more human than animal. And, if a gorilla stops smelling, the keeper starts worrying!

Tomas said that to his knowledge—and he was with them constantly—the gorillas were never turned loose in the same cage, although the cages were usually next to each other.

No attempt was made to mate them because they were considered too high strung and unpredictable, and circus officials didn't want to take a chance on either member of this valuable pair being injured, perhaps at play or in a fight.

Mrs. Hoyt, Tomas was quick to add, was very much attached to Toto and wouldn't hear of her being turned into the cage with the reputed reprobate next door!

The keeper scoffed at reports that Gargantua was deathly afraid of snakes, as was written many times. He also denied that he kept a small rubber snake in his pocket and used it to frighten the big ape, and send him scurrying from one part of the cage to another.

"He no afraid of snakes!" Tomas snorted. "He afraid of nothing! He only want to fight."

But he confirmed that both gorillas were terribly afraid of lightning and thunder, and when a storm came up, they'd shudder and run for cover.

Mrs. Lintz said time and again that "Buddy was not a wild gorilla but a captive," and Tomas said he found the two gorillas had entirely different personalities. Toto liked people and was pleased and happy when crowds gathered outside her cage.

"But Gargantua no like people," the keeper said. "He no like anything."

Tomas used to give Toto a blanket to play with and sleep on, so one day he gave one to Gargantua. He tore it to shreds the very first night. After that, Gargy got a new, cheap cotton blanket every night, and reduced it to strings. The circus bought them by the gross.

Gargantua sat in his glassed-in, air-conditioned cage and peered out at those who came to gawk at him.

Gargantua and M' Toto were exhibited in what was called "Gorilla Land," a menagerie tent set up near the Big Top.

The gorillas liked to watch each other, and when Toto did something, Gargantua would do the same. They were both great imitators.

"All gorillas same," Tomas said. "Man who feeds him all right, he like; the other man he want to kill!"

Henderson, the circus doctor, said once Gargantua had acute constipation, so he filled a Coke bottle with three ounces of castor oil and three ounces of Coca-Cola.

He slipped this through the bars to the ailing gorilla, who grasped the bottle and gulped down the contents. Old Gargy was in foul humor for days and never like the doctor after that, but it relieved his constipation!

CHAPTER ELEVEN

"Best Old Slob in the World"

When Gargantua the Great was introduced to American circus audiences in the 1938 season, he was wheeled around the hippodrome track in his air-conditioned, glass-enclosed cage while the announcer made his spiel.

After a couple of seasons, this was discontinued, and Mr. and Mrs. Gargantua the Great were exhibited in the menagerie tent, spending about eight months each year on the road and four in winter quarters.

During World War II, the gorillas were used in a highly successful campaign, selling millions of dollars worth of war bonds. For this effort, they received a special citation from high government officials in Washington.

The circus claimed Gargantua the Great weighed 650 pounds, but this was press agent talk. Dr. Henderson put his weight at "well over 550 pounds." Both were guesses. Nobody ever put old Gargy on the scales.

In the final years of his life, Gargantua the Great began to age visibly. His old coat of coarse black hair was speckled with gray, giving him a sort of silvery color. His eyes sank deeper under the bushy brows, and he spent the greater part of his time sitting or sleeping.

Mrs. Lintz told of one of her last visits with the old fellow when the circus was playing Madison Square Garden. She found him asleep, lying on his back with his legs in the air, the way he always slept.

She said she went close to the window and called him, and the big ape roused, got to his feet, ambled across the cage, and crouched down as close to her as he could get.

"For a full minute he gazed into my eyes with that steady, searching gaze of his, convincing himself that this was Missy, and that only love and pity were in her eyes.

"We couldn't hear each other, but I could see him mouthing his name for me. Then he got to his feet and beat his breast in delight. I have never had a sweeter tribute from my household, but what followed tore my heartstrings.

"He crouched down again, as close to me as he could get, and with one finger pulled up his scarred lip. He had a gumboil over one of his last baby teeth, and he had confided his trouble to none of his keepers. But he knew I wouldn't let him have an ache in his mouth, or anywhere in his great body, if I could help it.

"Now all I could do was to report the sore tooth, and go home. There was nothing I could do about Buddy's troubles any more, especially the biggest one of all—his life sentence in that luxurious jail of his.

"Unless he can find something to feed his mind and to make his life bearable, he will only fall deeper into a hopeless melancholia. I am afraid that he is slowly going mad."

Gargy was a trouper to the end, playing listlessly with his tire and swing, sneering at the men, women, and children who came to gaze at him. In his final days, he was visibly ailing, and spent most of his time huddled in a corner, suffering from a variety of ills no one could attempt to cure.

By now World War II had ended; I had been discharged from U.S. Navy duty and had gone to work for the Associated Press in the Miami bureau. I'd seen Gargy many times over the years, and I saw him during his final appearance on the night of Thursday, November 24, 1949.

For years he had been an active, vigorous specimen, but now he appeared to be an exhausted old creature, a dirty gray instead of rich black, curled up like a kitten on the floor in a corner. When I called his name, he never stirred or batted an eye.

"I've never seen him like this," I said to my friends. "If he's not asleep, he's a very sick gorilla. I just hope he lasts out the season."

But the poor old fellow never quite made it. The final performance was to be on Friday night, November 25, but at eight o'clock that morning, Gargantua the Great was found dead in his cage.

He had lived in captivity for about nineteen years, less than half the normal life span for a gorilla, the experts said. Twelve of those years had been spent in a glass and steel prison, with no unfiltered air, no outside noises, and no chance of escape.

E. V. W. Jones, day editor of the Associated Press in Miami at the time, received a tip that Gargantua was dead and immediately telephoned the Coral Gables police department for confirmation.

It was and still is A.P. policy to confirm such stories before they go on the

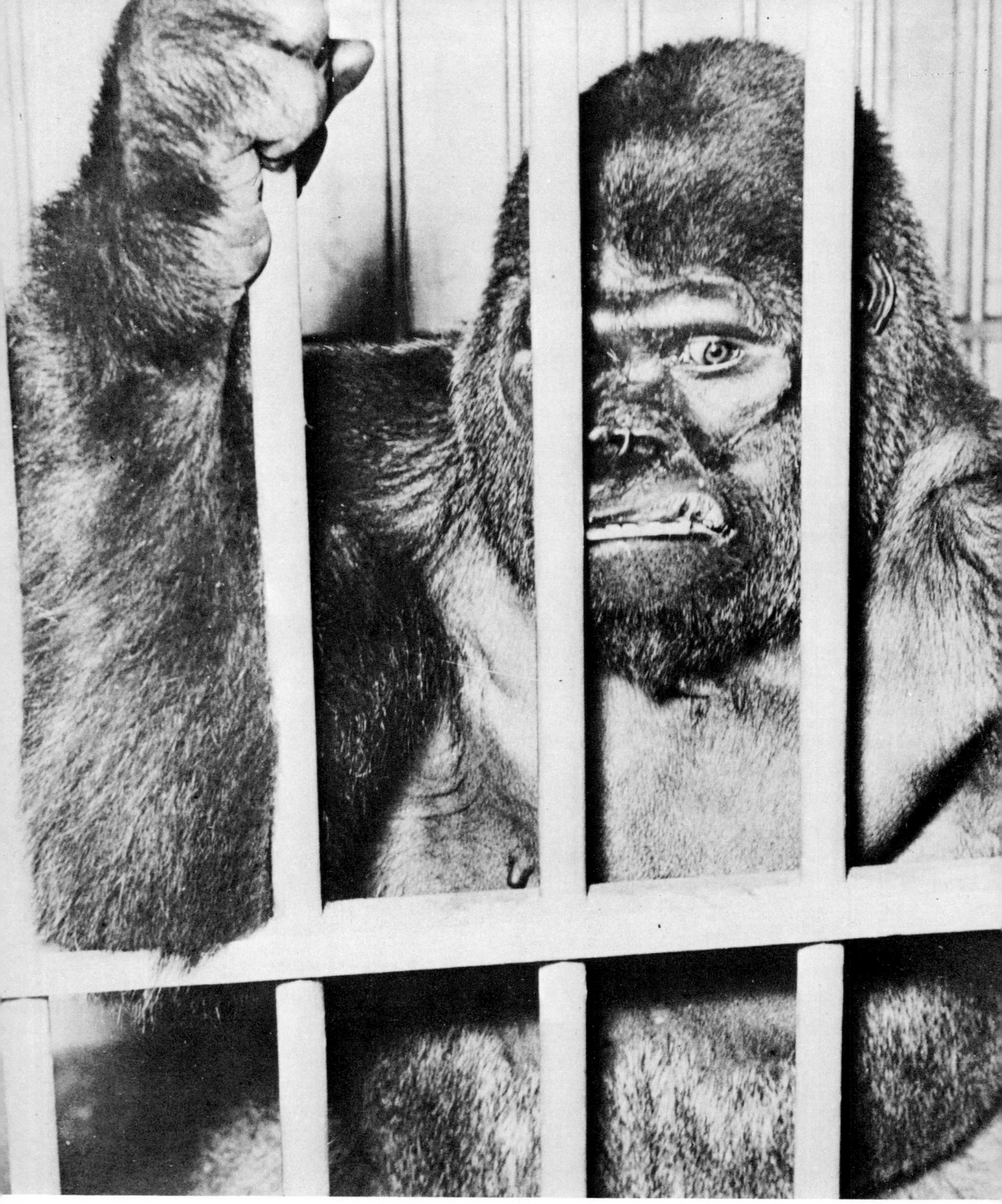

As the years rolled on, Gargantua the Great became a silver gray, but lost none of his vicious look. This is one of the last photographs made of the great gorilla.

wires. Although the circus was not in the city of Coral Gables, its tents were pitched just outside, on a large lot less than one mile from police headquarters. It was the nearest and most reliable source, and luck was with Eddie Jones.

"Yes sir," said a police officer in answer to his question. "I've just come in from out there. Gargantua is dead."

Jones asked a few other pertinent questions, then yelled to an operator seated at the teleprinter. The latter quickly broke into a story moving on the main trunk wire, and sent this momentous message:

FLASH

GARGANTUA DEAD

Such transcendent treatment was reserved for news of the utmost urgency—earth-shaking events like "War declared," "Roosevelt dead," "Truman wins," and the like.

Jones was a veteran newsman, and in his mature judgment, Gargantua's passing was of nationwide if not worldwide interest. It probably was the only time in its long history that the death of an animal was flashed on the Associated Press' national wire.

The dramatic announcement was followed immediately by a bulletin, bulletin matter, and several additions, giving complete details of the famous gorilla's life and death.

Gargantua was found dead in his cage while the circus was playing at Miami, Fla. Shown with the body are Henry Ringling North, who named Gargantua, and Jose Tomas, the keeper.

United Press got the story moments later, and its wires soon hummed with a complete account, written by Robert Vermillion, Miami bureau manager at the time and now an editor of *Newsweek* magazine.

International News Service, with James Russell in charge at Miami, carried the story to its clients throughout the world.

Within the hour, stories and pictures of Gargantua the Great flowed into newspaper offices around the world. Every radio station in the country—television was just beginning—had the news within minutes.

The *Miami News,* afternoon newspaper, bannered the story on page one, and gave a complete account, with a front page picture.

The *Miami Herald* used a three-column head and two-column picture on page one, with the story by Lawrence Thompson, one of its star reporters. The story was continued on an inside page, with a five-column picture of Gargantua's body in his cage, and a three-column picture of crowds around Mme. Toto's quarters.

On the same day Gargantua died, the wire services carried the story that Bill (Bojangles) Robinson, seventy-one-year-old star of stage and screen, had passed away of a heart ailment in a New York hospital.

Robinson was one of the country's greatest tap dancers; his twinkling toes and big heart made him one of show business' best-loved figures, the A.P. story said. But his passing did not receive the "flash" treatment accorded Gargy.

Also on that day occurred the death of J. C. Walton, a former governor of Oklahoma, and long-time foe of the Ku Klux Klan. Walton's death was duly reported, of course, but again there was no trunk wire "flash."

Many editors noted that while the Associated Press carried a "flash" on Gargantua's death, it did not give Robinson's passing such priority, perhaps one reason being that he was known to have been ill.

While Robinson's career spanned many years, he was a well-known and very popular show business figure, his death did not have quite the impact Gargantua's did, in the opinion of many qualified newsmen.

Merits of the news handling that day were debated at great length, both editorially and at conventions and symposiums. For months it was a prime topic of conversation wherever reporters and editors gathered.

Most agreed that Jones had acted as any good newsman should and had shown sound judgment, that Gargantua the Great had been seen alive through more eyes of people of all ages than any other circus attraction, or of any human being on earth up to that time.

tonight.

The Miami Herald

Saturday, November 26, 1949 No. 358 Florida's Most Complete Newspaper 39th Year 36 Pages 5 Cents

Minded Kentucky Tops Miam

med Gorilla 'Happy' To the End

Gargantua Dies In Miami With A Snarl On His Face

See pictures on Page 1-B

LAWRENCE THOMPSON
Herald Staff Writer

Gargantua The Great — the st famous and the meanest rilla in the world—died in ami Friday morning.

His still warm body was found his air-conditioned cage by keeper, Jose Tomas, at 8 . He was lying on his stomach, snarl on his face, indicating t he died happy, for he was ppy only when he was snarl- and mean.

And in the adjoining cage, sto, his wife, played happily th an orange, wearing hat would pass for a smile gorilla circles.

or although Gargantua's de- e was mourned by his owner, Ringling Bros. and Barnum d Bailey circus, and by the 000,000 people who have wed him, there was no sorrow the heart of the wife who spised him in life and disre- rded him in death.

Gargantua was 18 or 19 years —the exact date of his birth the Cameroons, West Africa, unknown.

The cause of death—those who ew him think it was cancer tuberculosis—will be deter- ned from an autopsy at Johns pkins medical center, Balti- re, by Prof. Adolph Schultz. rangements were made by f. Robert Yerkes, head of the partment of comparative anat- y at Yale University.

After that, Gargantua will be ffed and presented to the

GARGANTUA THE GREAT . . . found dead in air-conditioned cage

Many On Job

UN Rejects Vishinsky's Peace Plan

American-British Proposal Adopted; West Wins Victory By Record Margin

By The Associated Press

LAKE SUCCESS, N. Y.—The United Nations Friday beat down decisively a Soviet peace plan which carried a clause accusing the United States and Britain of preparing for a third world war.

Then, by 53 votes to 5, the United Nations approved a counter American-British program for peace.

The margin for the American-British proposal was the biggest the West has ever received in the United Nations on a major question. The Russian bloc of five stood alone against it and Yugoslavia abstained.

The heart of Soviet Foreign Minister Andrei Y. Vishinsky's proposal was knocked out 41 to 6 in the 59-nation political committee. Arab Yemen alone voted with the Moscow group in favor of a section calling on the United States, Britain, France, China and the Soviet Union to draw up a pact of peace. The fight will be renewed finally in the assembly proper, but there was no prospect of a change in the voting.

Vishinsky's attack on Britain and America, in the first paragraph of his resolution, was beaten by 52 votes to 5, with Yemen and Yugoslavia abstaining.

U.S. To Withhold Arias Recognit

Washington Shocked By Coup Assembly OK Former Preside

By The Associated Press

PANAMA CITY, Panama — Dr. Arnulfo Arias, late dent in Panama's dizzying series of coups, named a cab day night.

The United States announced curtly it has no di relations with the new regime.

This little Central American republic's third president in six days, the fiery, 49-year-old surgeon, selected his ministers and denied he is anti-American.

The big question here is whether Col. Jose Remon, the police chief who installed Arias, will remain in office now that the new president has been proclaimed by Congress.

Remon's action amazed Panama.

He and Arias had been bitter enemies since 1941, when the police chief ousted him as president. The police are this nation's only armed force, and he who heads the police wields power.

Remon and his sub-chiefs publicly told Arias their positions are at the president's disposal. Arias did not comment.

How Arias will fare without United States recognition remains to be seen. The United States did not formally break relations with this country, which is bisected by the strategic Panama Canal.

Assistant Secretary of State Edward G. Miller simply announced to a Washington news conference that the present United States ambassador here, Monnett Davis,

is accredited to a go "which no longer exists. pressed the United Stat found shock" at what h disregard of duly elected in Panama.

The Washington a ment apparently is a pr inter-American consulta recognition of the new in the light of recent he agreements concerning ments installed by force

Washington apparent move slowly, anxious to action which could be as interference with Par ternal affairs, and a del consultations is expected while, "no question of a the security of the canal raised," Miller reported.

The dispute over the p began Saturday night wi tempt by then Presiden Chanis to fire Col. Remon ges of involvement wit monopolies.

Instead of quitting, Re rounded the presidentia with his police and Chanis to resign.

Remon installed his c

Turn To Page 4-A, C

The Miami Herald *treated Gargantua's death as front page news on November 26, 1949, with a picture of the famous ape.*

MIAMI DAILY NEWS

Today's News Today ★ *Associated Press* ★ *United Press* ★ *AP Wirephotos* ★ *International News Service*

VOL. LIV., No. 299 PHONE 3-1191 MIAMI 30, FLA., FRIDAY EVENING, NOVEMBER 25, 1949 Entered as Second Class Matter At The Postoffice, Miami, Florida FIVE CENTS

GARGANTUA DIE

Two Bowl Bids Up To Wildcats

BY GUY BUTLER
Miami Daily News Sports Editor

Miami's Orange Bowl has a rival for the "hand" and "foot" (ball) of University of Kentucky, it developed today.

That would be the Cotton Bowl in Dallas.

Information came through that the Cotton had practically given up on Oklahoma, seemingly destined for the Sugar Bowl at New Orleans, and was casting around for a likely foe. Its gaze has fastened upon Kentucky's Wildcats, who are in town for their final battle of the regular season against the Hurricanes tonight in the stadium.

The story here is that the winner will step into the Orange Bowl against Santa Clara, with one proviso: Kentucky must whip Miami convincingly to win the award. On the other hand, the Hurricanes can eke out one over the Wildcats and still capture the invitation on its record (then) of seven victories in eight starts.

* * *

It was learned, however, that Kentucky isn't altogether restricted to a possible Orange Bowl bid, that the Cotton has put out a strong feeler. And that if it gives U-M a lacing it might well wind up in Dallas where they pay some $30,000 more than the Orange Bowl committee, which has a ceiling of $75,000 per team.

Bear Bryant, coach of the Kentuckians, was understood to be giving both bowls considerable thought.

Jack Roche, scout for Santa Clara, arrived in Miami this afternoon to take a look at the two teams, one of which may draw the assignment of facing the Broncos in the Jan. 2 Orange Bowl game.

Oklahoma and Tulane in the Sugar Bowl seems the logical match, especially if the Green Wave blasts LSU tomorrow. Rice or Baylor will be the defending champion in the Cotton Bowl, but who will be its cpponent? There's the rub. And it might turn out to be Kentucky.

* * *

Indeed, the Wildcats could conceivably wind up being sought by all three of the still-open major bowls—if Tulane is licked by Louisiana State, its arch rival, and that is not stretching it too far for the Bayou Bengals are rated about even with Tulane for this contest.

Thus, if the Greenies are whipped, despite their just-won Southeastern Conference championship New Orleans

See Butler Page 4A Col. 4

92-Day Fast Is Fatal To Pole Sitter

BIRMINGHAM, Ala., Nov. 25—(AP)—Percy Copion, who started what he said would be a 100-day fast on Aug. 25, died early today.

Percy, a jocular five-by-five who weighed 357 pounds at the start, had gone 92 days without food. His weight had dropped to 245 pounds.

He was 53.

Copion spent most of the fast in a small house atop a 30-foot pole at his home. Last Sunday he came down because of dissines and said he would finish his 100-day fast in his home.

His dizziness diminished and Percy was in good spirits yesterday. He lapsed into unconsciousness just before midnight, however, falling to the floor in his bathroom.

Two physicians worked over him but he died during the night.

Percy told reporters at the start of his fast that he hoped to prove that human body can heal itself without medicine if it is gien the chance. He said he was not undertaking the long fast to gain publicity.

As his waistline receded, Percy joked with reporters. He had announced he would begin taking food next week, starting with a spoon of orange juice.

Philippine Pilots Bomb Rebels

MANILA, Nov. 25—(AP)—Constabulary headquarters expressed the opinion rebels holed up in the mountains of Batangas province today suffered "great slaughter" in a combined air, artillery and ground attack by government forces.

Planes in repeated sorties strafed and bombed the rebel positions. A joint army, navy and constabulary offensive was ordered by President Elpidio Quirino. Three Manilla newspapers deplored the order.

GARGANTUA, FAMOUS CIRCUS GORILLA IS DEAD
Giant Ringling Bros. Attraction Died During Early Morning Hours

Ape's Lif… On Last D… Big Top S…

Holiday Death Toll In Nation Climbs To 161

CHICAGO, Nov. 25—(AP)—The nation's death toll in violent accidents over the Thanksgiving day holiday was one of the highest in several years.

There were at least 161 violent deaths from 6 p.m. Wednesday to midnight Thursday. These included 103 traffic fatalities. Fifty-eight persons died in miscellaneous accidents, including fires, plane crashes, shootings, falls and hunting. Also included were 14 persons killed in Alabama tornadoes.

This year's Thanksgiving violent deaths compared to 114 …

Mad Dog Killer Loses Last Plea

CHICAGO, Nov. 25—(AP)— A federal district judge today refused to intervene in the scheduled execution of James Morelli, "mad dog" killer.

Morelli has been ordered to die in the electric chair early tomorrow. Police patrolled the Cook county jail as a result of a thwarted attempt by two young men to free him.

Federal Judge Philip K. Sullivan dismissed a petition for habeas corpus on behalf of Morelli, filed by his wife, Genevieve. The dismissal came just 13 hours before the 23 year old killer's minute-after-midnight date in the chair.

His attorneys said they will appeal Judge Sullivan's decision to the federal district court of appeals.

Navy Proves It's Superior Of Sub Packs

WASHINGTON, Nov. 25—(UP) — The navy is readying some …

The Miami News *also bannered Gargantua's death on its front page the day he died and carried a full account of the gorilla's life.*

"There was only one Jumbo and only one Gargantua," said John Ringling North in a statement announcing the death of his famous gorilla.

During its final two performances on that Friday, there was a distinct air of sadness about the circus, particularly on the back yard, where workmen paused and passed the word about "old Gargy."

When Merle Evans and his band played the traditional "Auld Lang Syne" that night, tears filled the eyes of performers and patrons alike, not only for the end of the tour but for the passing of the sneering but lovable old star in the fur coat.

Some reporters included in their stories the observation that Mme. Toto, who had trouped with Gargantua for nine seasons, was aware of his death and appeared depressed.

"He was no stranger to Toto," Tomas explained. "They lived right next door. Toto was never turned loose in the cage with him, but they were neighbors. She was very grieved, very sad. When Gargantua died, she was all alone."

North, in an attempt to keep the gorilla attraction alive, and to comfort Mme. Toto, acquired two young gorillas which the circus billed as "Mademoiselle Toto and Gargantua II." One was a female about eight months old and twenty inches tall; the other was a male twelve months old and two feet tall, the circus said.

But Gargantua the Great was gone, and from that day on, the great Ringling Bros. and Barnum & Bailey Combined Shows was never quite the same. Times had changed, and the circus must change, too.

After the passing of Gargantua the Great, Mme. Toto trouped with the show only in Madison Square Garden, spending the rest of the year in winter quarters. The circus moved its headquarters to Venice, Florida, in the fall of 1959, and it was there that Mme. Toto—Mrs. Gargantua the Great—died on July 17, 1968.

The circus was on tour at the time, and the event was noted in a brief news story, transmitted in routine fashion by the wire services, much in the same manner of the death of the widow of a famous man.

Mme. Toto had not been ill, Tomas recalled recently, and the day before she died, she ate her food as usual and drank all her milk. She was then a fairly old gorilla, having passed her thirty-sixth birthday. Mrs. Hoyt said she was born about November, 1931.

Tomas was puzzled when his charge refused to eat breakfast on the final morning.

"I went into her cage," he remembers. "She didn't want her milk—

nothing. She looked very sleepy. It was then about ten o'clock, and she would not eat. I tried again at eleven o'clock. This time she was more sleepy than before. She died in my arms—died of old age—just went to sleep in my arms."

Tomas was heartbroken, as was Mrs. Hoyt, her owner and almost constant companion all her life. Both grieved as anyone would for a dear pet. Mrs. Hoyt was living in Sarasota at the time, and went to see Toto every day.

When her beloved gorilla died, Mrs. Hoyt made arrangements for the funeral, and Mme. Toto was buried in a pet cemetery in Sarasota. Mrs. Hoyt arranged for fresh flowers to be placed on the grave every day, as long as she lived.

Tomas said Toto weighed about 400 pounds when he played with her at the Hoyt home in Cuba, and later got up to 575, which just about matched the avoirdupois of Baby Ruth, Baby Irene, and other fat ladies featured in the Ringling sideshow.

Gargantua's best friend, Mrs. Gertrude Davies Lintz, spent her final years in Florida. She bought a four-acre place at Ojus, north of Miami, and she acquired another gorilla, which she sold to Dr. Yerkes.

Mrs. Lintz died in a hospital in North Miami on Labor Day, 1968, but her passing went unreported in the press. Friends say her husband, who died a couple of years later, would not permit it.

Marie Hoyt, who liked to travel, was fatally injured in an automobile accident in Vienna while on a European tour in 1969.

When Gargantua the Great died, his body was packed in dry ice and sent to Johns Hopkins Hospital in Baltimore, where an autopsy was performed and studies made to determine what had killed him, and to learn as much as possible about the famed gorilla.

Maligned and misunderstood all his life, scarred and imprisoned by man, stared and hissed at by millions who believed he was the meanest monster on earth, Gargantua the Great died of bilateral (double) pneumonia complicated by a skin disease, four completely impacted and rotted wisdom teeth, and other ailments.

"Gargantua died because of his distrust and viciousness," said Dr. Henderson. "His outstanding characteristics prevented his friends from helping him, and eventually killed him. The real tragedy of a gorilla is that his disease may be curable, but the patient himself is untreatable."

His skeleton was sent to the Peabody Museum at Yale University. Henry Ringling North, a Yale graduate who had named the ape and was one of his admirers, commented that "Gargantua always was a Yale man."

In this fine character study, M' Toto might be called the grieving widow. Her keeper, Jose Tomas, said she knew Gargantua was gone and she grieved for him.

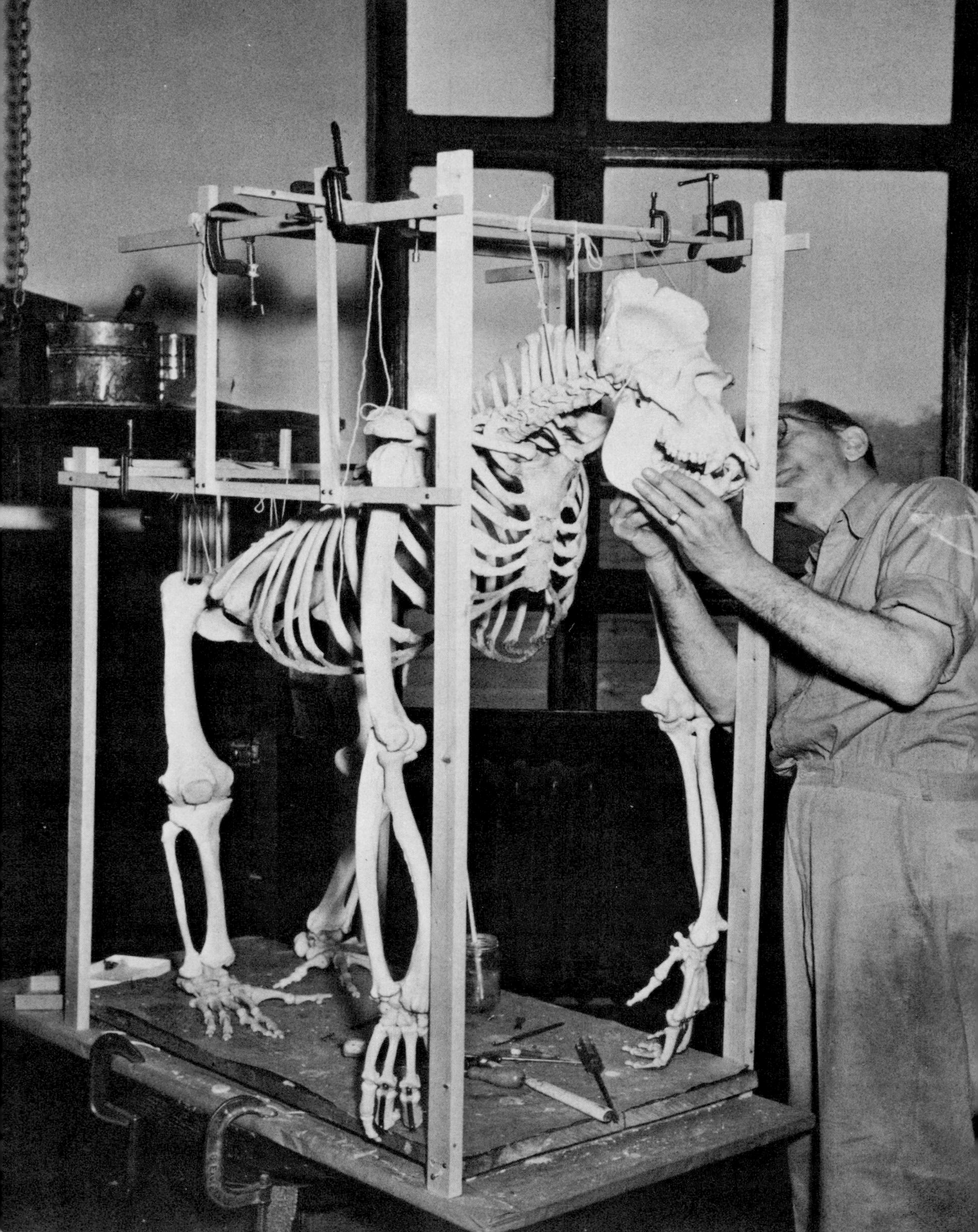

Dr. S. Dillon Ripley, curator of vertebrate zoology at the Peabody Museum, wrote me shortly after the gorilla died.

"Gargantua was by no means the largest of twenty-three gorillas in captivity," the scientist said. "That was circus publicity. Nor was he the oldest. He was five feet seven and one-half inches tall, and weighed 312 pounds."

His foot, Dr. Ripley added, would have filled a size 12 DDDD shoe, and his hand could have been squeezed into a size 11 glove.

His measurements still exceeded those of the average college or professional football player, and coaches, admiring his massive shoulders and long arms, invariably sighed wistfully, "What a great guard or tackle he might have made!"

Expressions of sorrow poured into the circus when the old star died, and circus-goers everywhere recalled how they had stood outside his cage and been thrilled as they stared in childish wonder at the great shaggy beast whose deep-set, yellowish eyes seemed to be peering at them, his mouth twisted in a fiendish, chilling sneer.

Over the years, many animal lovers actually had a feeling of affection, admiration, or at least sympathy for the hairy old fellow known affectionately around the circus as "Gargy."

Perhaps the most appropriate and touching tribute to the greatest circus star of them all came from the one person who had known and loved him since childhood, his warm admirer and close friend—Mrs. Gertrude Davies Lintz.

"He was the best old slob in the world," she said.

Gargantua's skeleton being assembled at Peabody Museum, Yale University, where it was placed on display as a gift from Henry Ringling North, circus official and Yale graduate.

Index